The Big Book About Sounds

Sounds You Can Hear,
Sounds You Can't Hear,
and
Sounds You Won't Hear

Alan Herbert Rowan Baptiste Barysh,
M.E.O.B.

Available as an ebook
ISBN 978-1-968640-02-6 (Paperback)
ISBN 978-1-968640-03-3 (Hardcover)

Publify Publishing
Lampasas, TX 76550
contact@publifypublishing.com

CONTENTS

DEDICATION

IT IS WITH PROFOUND RESPECT THAT THIS EFFORT IS DEDICATED TO :

(IN SOME KIND OF ALPHABETICAL ORDER)

1) KAY ADLER FOR GIVING ME ALL THE ADVICE I NEED TO SURVIVE

2) AMANDA ARMSTRONG FOR HELPING ME GET SOME SKIN IN THE GAME

3) SUE AND ADRIAN AKERMAN FOR EVERYTHING THAT MAKES A FRIEND A FRIEND

4) ANN BARYSH (MY LOVING SISTER) -FOR BEING MY FRIEND AND SUPPORT

5) JONATHAN BROWN FOR HELPING ME STAY RED

6) PAIGE BACON FOR KEEPING ME IN GOOD HEALTH

7) ANDRE "BUTCH BOBBIT" FOR TELLING ME ALL I NEED TO KNOW ABOUT PRINTING

8) MATTHEW LLOYD CAUFFMAN FOR JUST BEING THE DUDE

9) KENNETH CARROLL FOR REMINDING ME THAT I WAS NOT CRAZY-I WAS LIVING IN AMERICA

10) GRACE CAVALIERI FOR JUST BEING A GOOD FRIEND WHEN I NEEDED IT URGENTLY

11) IN ALPHABETICAL ORDER

12) ALLISON DIETZ, AMY DIETZ, BENJAMIN DIETZ, CAROLINE DIETZ, CAROLINE DIETZ, EMILY DIETZ, GRACE DIETZ, GREGORY DIETZ, JULIA DIETZ, LILLIAN DIETZ, WILLIAM DIETZ

13) MINAS CONSOLAS FOR GIVING ME A PLACE TO READ

14) ALICE LIEM FOR NOT WINCING WHEN I TELL A REAL GROANER

15) ANDRE AND LAUREL MENDEZ, WHO WALK THE WALK AND TALK THE TALK WHEN IT COMES TO FEEDING THE HOMELESS

16) LINDA RICHARDSON FOR GIVING ME A PLACE TO READ ALOUD

17) CECE ROSE FOR STAYING RED

18) CINDY AND JEFF SWISS, IT WOULD TAKE BOOKS TO TELL YOU ALL ABOUT THEM

19) Michael Tolson TENTATIVELY a CONVIENCE. You name it-I'm grateful to him

20) AND ANYONE ELSE THAT I FORGOT IN MY HURRY, I FORGOT TO GET THIS EFFORT OUT

Welcome to my book.

I hope you like it!

This is the real introduction

You are about to read a collection of essays on silence. Music, politics and much more. It is the latest reinvention of "Scrap Book Writing" and should you not be a pink boy/girl/snowflake/or woke you will in fact understand the ebb and flow of this project

Alan Herbert Rowan Baptiste Barysh MEOB

Baltimore, Maryland

8/15/25 12:47:20 AM

The "excess" of pictures is to create a sense of anxiety that has been captured quite well in the masterpiece movie Weekend by Jean Luc -Goddard. In that film there is a scene with a traffic jam that goes on and on and resolves itself with a scene of a horrific car crash. In other films Jean Luc -Goddard has used what in printing would be a "step and repeat " process to frustrate viewers and to let these images sink in. This is also true of John Cage who said in so many words the longer you look at a boring picture the less bored you will be.

Alan Herbert Rowan Baptiste Barysh MEOB

CHAPTER ONE

4/22/19 5:41 PM
<u>Scrap Book Writing</u>
<u>Ghost/Spirit Writing</u>
<u>Scroll Writing</u>
<u>And</u>
<u>Other Forms of Putting Words on Pages</u>

<u>By</u>
<u>Alan Barysh</u>

"Self-acceptance is terribly difficult and is, not that you asked, the primary obsession of mine. It is the ultimate sin, you'll find, to ignore or to deny who and what we are. As a human--tragedy. As an artist--insanity.

One's style, whatever that is, is simply the only way we can communicate or share. To apply a style, like a rancid batter, is folly. Tell your story in the only way you can. One of the most potent ways to discover and to accept yourself is to tell your story honestly. There you will find yourself."
--Harold Pinter/Interview with James Grissom/1997/

Another Introduction to Volume One And Two of Remembrance of Cookies Past
Scrap Book Writing and the Films of Jean Luc – Goddard and Others
Part One
An Over All View of The Parallel Developments in My Writing and the Films of Jean Luc Goddard
Or
Goddard Came First, I Just Found out About it

For Rupert Wondowliski

Lind Richardson

And

Kenneth Carrol

Who helped me keep my sanity, when Anselm Hollo and his friends were trying to steal it from me.

As I have been engaged in creating this scrapbook series, it has become extremely obvious to me, that a somewhat decent thing to do, would be doing a second introduction to this series might not be such a bad idea. With that in mind, I have undertaken to clarify what I feel is a new form of writing for me. At the same time that I have found that I have been watching more films by Jean Luc Goddard, and other directors. The strange thing is that I did not watch these movies, and say to myself:" Ahh, I can do that!" Instead, after watching a number of Goddard's films, I said to myself:" Whoa boy, *that's* where *I* want to go!" (With a few changes on my part) For example, the idea of characters talking directly to the viewer became part of my writing. The idea of quick jump cuts and flashy credit titles led to my changing fonts and the pagination in the first season of this book, and well into the first episode of the second season. The idea of putting politics of a beyond the pale into these books came directly into my mind, before I watched these films. With the exception of Hail Mary, I can't remember seeing any other Goddard film but Weekend. As a matter of fact, I cannot remember anything about Hail Mary. Weekend, however. stands out in my mind of a piece of cinematic genius. Even though it fails what I call "The Dietz Test"[1] by more than a country mile, I have managed to pull out some of the effects, and concepts. The viewer is drawn into a world that lays down the artistic gauntlet for all dystopian filmmakers. This decent into a hell where burning and trashed motor vehicles line the road as the main characters stumble their way towards their destination, still remains a vast resource that I can learn from. For example, the way the two garbage haulers speak directly to the

---

[1] More on this later.

audience, gives me the idea of writing as many ways as I can for injecting politics into the story. (Note: this idea goes back to the first Greek plays and thought to the writings of Berthold Brecht. For example, the ending of Three Penny Opera, The Rag Pickers soliloquy in Madwoman of Chaillot or the protagonist's principal's last speech in Breaking With Old Ideas are other examples of this Deus Ex Machina that have been used by others, so I am not saying I created anything new.)

However, I must say that after watching a number of Jean Luc Goddard's films, I became amazed that what I called "scrap book writing or the scrap book novel" was so pronounced in movies by this film maker that I have never seen, before writing the first volumes, or season one. When I saw the flashing of images, the mortgages woven into the films, I had to say out loud to myself "Dag Mr. B. this is what you have done in the printed word!" And, when I saw the monologues, and dialogues, and discussions between characters, that went on for quite a while, I saw what I was trying to recreate in my endeavors. Even in the first introduction, I found out that I needed to go into greater detail. Ten, there was one another thing that Jean Luc Goddard did, that I realized that I was doing. That was the introduction of politics, primary *revolutionary* politics into his films. These injections of politics were very close to mine. I remember watching British Sounds and holding my breath watching a bloody hand that looked like a sock puppet or the hand puppet of Senior Wenses crawling through the snow, as the narrator quoted a number of quotes from Quotations From Chairman Mao (AKA "The Little Red Book"). While I was not a blatant about this, I realized that I had done the same thing in my writing.

Senor Wences with Johnny his hand ...
pinterest.com

CHAPTER TWO

As I was saying I have been facing a challenge, let me tell you more

Part One
Introduction

For the longest time, I have been trying to free the words I have written from the rigid structures of the normal writing forms. Inn my first three books, Bugged, Slugged, and Mugged I tried doing this by putting sections in the various chapters. That was okay for then. I was quite happy with that *at that time*. However, I wanted something more. The poetry attempts I made were somewhat okay. However, I was looking for something that turned small envelopes into big ones. This year (2019) when I retired I started a five-volume series of pulp fiction books. (To be more exact *politically correct* pulp fiction books). I wrote the first paragraph with nothing in mind for what was to happen next. The story just unfolded. After writing the first few words, and saying good night, I resumed writing the next day. Gradually a plot with shifting plots developed. I wrote for two to three hours a day, only stopping, when I felt tired. Gradually, I began to realize I was on the verge of something that was new to me. It was so new, that I felt compelled to tell the reader what I was doing.

Now I have decided to codify these attempts in order to encourage other to try this style. So now let me begin.

As with any creative endeavor, one must acknowledge the influences that helped form the results of the work in making this vision come true. Since the basic influence is the composer John Cage, let us turn our attention to his music, my search for silence, and how this new concept presented itself to me.

Searching For Silence
Part One

<u>Away With All Social Realism[2]</u>

<u>OR</u>

<u>This Is Why A Lot of People Get Turned Off When Typical "Commies" Barely Can Even See Let Alone Barely See Beyond Their Nose When It Comes To Understanding Anything Seriously Artistic. Not Only That, But They Will Try And Brow Beat Anyone Who Has The Slightest Artistic Vision Into thinking Along Their "Party Line"</u>

<u>OR</u>

<u>Why did Shostakovich Sleep OUTSIDE HIS OWN Apartment?[3]</u>

Somewhere in the book Quotations From Chairman Mao (The "Little Red Book" to you) Mao says that if a work of art is dull artistically and correct politically, it's a bad piece of art. The same is true for any creative endeavor. That means that presentation should be of the utmost importance in the goal of the writer. However, a lot of people who claim to be political artists or "worker/artists" do not grasp this. To be quite frank, an artist, writer or whatever is someone who makes their living doing that. (Or at least aspires to do that.) This "worker/artist" hogwash should have been purged from the world outlook of leftists' decades ago. Instead, the dull heavy hand of Stalin as filtered through Earl Browder prevailed.

---

[2] Note this an excerpt from the book On Silence And Other Non-Sounds by this author. It is reprinted here exactly the way it appeared in that book-font and all. Note this was before your writer started referring to himself in the second person.

[3] Look it up somewhere! The question is posed-you do the legwork!

The result was seriously sad. For example, the songs of Woody Guthrie are for the most part dull hack jobs. Even though Joe Hill wrote a few good satires, they too are outdated artistically. The play Waiting For Lefty by Clifford Oddets cries out for a lot of editing. Listening to the Almanac Singers or the Weavers once made my spine shiver, not anymore. As much as I respect the courage of Paul Robeson, I find that his art and politics lacking. For example, I remember seeing a picture of Paul Robeson singing The Star-Spangled Banner with some striking miners. I remember getting a sick feeling in the pit of my stomach. I thought, why is a COMMUNIST singing that God-awful song *instead of the INTERNATIONALE?* Years later both Jimmi Hendrix and Carla Bley recorded better versions of that war mongering tune.

Then it dawned on me. The people who were upholding this hogwash *never* were the revolutionaries or communists they claimed to be. As if to prove me correct, I remember reading a quote by the then leader of the Communist Party USA Earl Browder who said something to the effect "Communism is twentieth century Americanism" Even though he was axed from his own party, the residual effects still remain. They still infect what some people call "the left" From "Art for the 99% to "people's art" the result is the same. Watered down pabulum. Movies like Norma Rae or Salt of The Earth become the nocturnal emissions of people who tail after mass movements the way shyster lawyers chase after ambulances. At this point The Workers World Party is a might good example of a bad trend. Every International Women's Day they trot out Salt of The Earth, Sing Union Maid have a brief self-promoting talk, eat some store-bought cookies and soda pop and go home. Gee whiz I thought they could have found better stuff.

What does this have to do with what I started out to say? It's simple. I was looking for something that was *both* revolutionary artistically *and* politically, and all I was coming up with was dead ends. This lasted on and off from my high school days to my retirement days, with a few wonderful momentary pauses.

I think the first break through was Edgar Varese.

End Piece[4]

"The reason I like staying up late so much is because between the hours of 1am to 5am the world is quiet and no one expects anything from me. I could literally stare at the wall for four hours with no consequences. I love the silence and calm. I love it "

B. McCoy

---

[4] Not in the original piece

Part Two
Edgar Varese to the Rescue

"Do not worry about what your friends say about my music. They listen with their memories only"

Edgar Varese in a letter to me

I cannot remember when it was, however one summer I went off to a summer camp called Buck's Rock Work Camp (sic). In the midst of being put down by even more spoiled offspring of upper petit bourgeois children I discovered the music of Edgar Varese. I believe that it was at a lecture by a composer by the name of Ralph Shapey. During his lecture he played what he called "electronic music" among the examples he played for this small group was the music of Edgar Varese. This was not only an eye-opening music; it was a soul opening experience. For the first time I heard music that was so daring that my spine just shivered, as it does every time I experience some kind of new music or writing or cinema

This was a liberation day. The music I heard had broken free of the dull music of music class. This was the answer to the endless hours of listening to endless recording of singer who wished to be Joan Baez. At last, there was an answer to those God-Awful Child songs. At last, I realized that I did not have to like those self-pitying songs like "all My Trials" and "I am a Man of Constant Sorrow" Sadly I was too early for blues, or rhythm and blues. I had skipped the rock and roll of the Everly Brothers, Jan and Dean ET all. The Kingston Trio and all those singers had by passed my radar. However, this was the music that made my folks yell: "For God's sake turn down *THAT* music!" That was heaven to me. Even after doing the folks a favor, I knew this was my music. That brown long-playing record with the Joan Miro painting on the cover, was my audio ticket out of my home. If the record was my ticket out, Poem Electronique was the engine that drove the train. From Varese I discovered Milhaud, Charles Ives, and Aaron Copeland, Mendelssohn, Mozart, Bach, and a whole host of others. The ABA pop song had been a whole new form of music. This was *listening to music*. This was *serious* music. This was music for real instruments, not the flute-a-phones and tambourines our music teacher foisted upon us in "music" class. And the "for God's sake turn down *THAT music* was the balm to my soul. As I have gone through my life from Varese to Dave Brubeck to Charlie Parker to Mingus to John Cage and on and on "*TURN DOWN THAT MUSIC!* could only mean one thing. *THIS* was the new sound I had to learn to appreciate.

"*TURN DOWN THAT MUSIC!* "

"*TURN DOWN THAT MUSIC!* "

"*TURN DOWN THAT MUSIC!* "

"*TURN DOWN THAT MUSIC!* "

These words were repeated in every house in the nation.

"*TURN DOWN THAT MUSIC!* "

It's the last gasp of a dying generation.

"TURN DOWN THAT MUSIC! "

and,

"Your sons and daughters are beyond your control" were the words those young folks loved to hear when we were searching for some sound that spoke to us.

"TURN DOWN THAT MUSIC! "

"TURN DOWN THAT MUSIC! "

"TURN DOWN THAT MUSIC! "

"TURN DOWN THAT MUSIC! "

Whether it was Elvis stealing Big Mamma Thornton's' Hound Dog

The Sherrill's "Please Mr. Postman"

Chuck Berry singing "Almost Grown'

Milton Babbitt's "All Set"

Lady Day

Bird

Mingus

Carla Bley

When a rebel youth hears

"TURN DOWN THAT MUSIC! "

They know that for a brief period of time *THEY* are in control of the environment in their home!

THEY called the shots!

THEY struck horror into the hearts of THE GROWN UPS!

"TURN DOWN THAT MUSIC! "

"TURN DOWN THAT MUSIC! "

"TURN DOWN THAT MUSIC! "

"TURN DOWN THAT MUSIC! "

May those words echo in the minds of children, who are now adults, who have replaced those words with

"PUMP UP THE VOLUME"

"PUMP UP THE VOLUME"

"PUMP UP THE VOLUME"

"PUMP UP THE VOLUME"

What does this have to do with silence?

It's not that simple. Let me elaborate. In spite of the obvious fact that the love of music played at a loud volume was the desire of the new generation, there always a sub text. That sub text was the respect for silence. Yes, as rebel youth we loved listening to the later versions of John Coltrane or Art Blakey, or The Velvet Underground, we also listened to the quiet music. Whenever we listened to an arco bass played by Charles Mingus with raped attention. We understood that after a spirited performance of Albert Ayler, it was obvious there was a need for silence before the applause broke out. The more that curious listeners listened loud well-orchestrated music a somewhat begrudging respect for silence began to develop. Speaking for myself I have begun to think that silence has in fact enables a more robust form of music to bloom. You will realize this to. Silence, or to be more correct the absence of organized sound is the equivalent to the canvas an artist uses to paint on. It doesn't matter that the viewer sees the canvas. What is true that every viewer who looks at a painting knows that the paint is on a blank canvas. In the back of the mind of music listeners is the tacit knowledge that organized sound is filling up the place where the absence of organized sound had previously occupied. However, how many of us realize the strategic need to cherish silence. Silence gives us the power to listen. Silence gives a reason to appreciate what organized sound we have just been listening to. How many times have the phrase been said "It's so loud in here that *I can't hear myself think*"? That phrase is the expression of a desire to listen to something covered up by the over presence of organized sound. I can't hear myself think expresses a desire for the searcher to look inward and outward for a place where contemplative may present themselves to the listeners.

I remember once listening to a record album by the Beach Boys. I believe it was the recording with the name Having A Party With The Beach Boys. The last song on the album was Barbra Ann. This version was no better or worse than any other Beach Boys recording (Except for Pet Sounds). In the last few seconds of the song the Beach Boys started goofing off. The ending was a faux operettic climax. When the last silly off key high notes left the air, there was a silence. Then for some odd reason I became aware that the tone arm had lifted the needle of the record. Then there was a bit more unorganized sound. This unorganized sound was broken by a sharp clicking sound, signifying the record player had turned itself off. I lay there on my couch listening to the environment of the living room. Then the importance of listening to unorganized sound was the key factor to my understanding of organized sound,

A week later I was talking to a friend about this very same Beach Boys album. My friend informed me the album was in fact was a studio recording set up to sound like a spontaneous jam session at a party. This made me think of the classic recording Mingus Presents Mingus. On this album, Charles Mingus pretends the ensemble he is working with is in a night club. In the introduction of the record and the introduction to various songs Mr. Mingus asks for complete silence. (At one point he says something to the effect "don't rattle the ice in the glasses. Later he says, "Thank you again for *not* applauding." While on the surface it might be seen as the anger the composer felt when people were talking over the music of his ensembles when they performed in the various and sundry venues, there was something else going on. This revelation obvious at it is -is this. Organized in the form of music sound needs the absence of conflicting organized in the form of useless chit chat and pointless ambient sounds created by cash register noise and tinkling ice cubes and other distractions in order to be heard and appreciated.

A few years later the singing duo did what years of silence advocation by John Cage could never do. They recorded a hit called THE SOUNDS OF SILENCE. Then at that point it was obvious that unorganized sound had come into its own. A few years later, Andy Warhol put a contribution on a compilation ESP recording Just like the Beach Boys did on their Party Album, Mr. Warhol had his bit put on the end of the album The effect of hearing the machine click off was the same. Andy Warhol had discovered the beauty of unorganized sound A while later. The first electric Miles

Davis album recorded, IN A SILENT WAY reaffirmed the vital role of unorganized sound. I do not know when the Carla Bley recording Escalator Over The Hill was recorded. However, at the end of this recording there is at least twenty-five minutes of unorganized sound. The great alto saxophonist Anthony Braxton recorded an album called For Alto. He dedicates a piece of music to John Cage. The lack of organized sound is just lovely. As a matter of fact, this was the composition that truly made me appreciate the genius of John Cage. If it were not for Ralph Shapey making me aware of Edgar Varese I might be trying to figure out what real music was all about.

"It is better to be silent than to dispute with the ignorant"

Pythagoras

"Don't ever be ashamed of loving the strange things that make your little heart happy"

Elizabeth Gilbert.

"Do not worry about what your friends think of my music. They listen with their memories only"

Edgar Varese in a letter to this author

CHAPTER THREE

Part Three
But You Have To Them/Him /Her Live

"When you are on stage you have a very strange knowledge of what the audience it isn't exactly a sound-it's a hum"

Keith Jarrett

Every once in a while, when in a discussion about the latest recorded presentation of a composer or a recording group, someone will say as if on que: "Ah but you have to hear them/him/her live!" For the listener who has become aware of the existence of the presence of unorganized sound, this rings especially true. Try this the next time you go to hear/see organized sound in the form of music. Before you start listening to the performance start listening. Do you hear sounds of feet shuffling? Can you hear instruments tuning up? Is that the sound of a hushed conversation? Are traffic sounds filtering into the venue? If there is a restaurant or café in there can you hear kitchen sounds. Cooking sounds, plate sounds? When the listener that becomes aware of the presence of unorganized sound everywhere they go, it becomes obvious that this savvy listener will get a greater appreciation of organized musical sounds, as well as the sounds of life all around the ears of the listener. And, if the observant listener really listens, they can imagine hearing the sounds of the composer or performer thoughts during the performance.

Whether the listener takes the time to listen to the unorganized sounds during a live performance or not, the joy of seeing live organized sounds should last a lifetime. I remember going to a concert where the cartridge music of John Cage was performed and enjoying it as much as listing to All Set being performed by Milton Babbit. The baritone saxophone solos Trevor Lawrence with Paul Butterfield are happy memories as are the foot tapping sounds of Charles Mingus on the recording Mingus at Monterey. The things that unite these musical memories is not only the organized musical sounds these composers created, but the fact that all the other disorganized sounds of the universe gave the organized sounds a place to grow and thrive.

Part Four Three
What About Space?

If as John Cage pointed out to the world, silence does not exist. Silence is the absence of organized sound, what then, can be said of space? The answer is obvious to the observer. There is no such thing as space. "Space" or "Open Space" as we call it is not "space". "Space" is merely the absence of clearly recognized organized forms. Just as the existence of sounds that are inaudible to the *human* ear is not some made up story, so the existence of objects and colors that are not detectable to human vision is a natural fact. The existence of objects and colors beyond the scope of human vision does in my opinion give the viewer a sense of depth perspective.

Take this example. The average driver knows just by looking how far away the car they are driving is away from the next car or stop light. The existence of unseen objects that the driver might readily see might aid in giving the driver a sense of perspective. This is also true of colors. A sunset or sunrise reveals more than just colors. These events also act as a prelude to the advancing or retreating of light. Sometimes it takes the viewer a bit of time to in the words of the pop song "Guess Who I Saw Today?" have the eyes get "adjusted to the gloom." Having the eyes get adjusted to "the gloom" gave the protagonist a chance to spot her unfaithful husband. Extrapolating from this theory one could say that had the viewer been born with a better type of vision, then after her eyes got "adjusted to the gloom" she might have seen other microscopic forms

The Big Book About Sounds

around her. The point is and I paraphrase Bob Avakian Chairman of the Revolutionary Communist Party "You can't see germs, but you sure can catch them when you get a cold" During the Great Proletarian Cultural Revolution in China the concept of needing both a telescope, and a microscope to analyze the world became part and parcel of the efforts to transform the old feudal society into a new society. This also is a good method of learning and practice for the person involved in the creative process. You need a telescope of the imagination to see where and how you want your endeavors to go. You need a microscope to find the flaws in your creations, so that they may in fact have wings and lives of their own and go in the direction you wish them to go. With this part over, I will now go into some detail about this has influenced my writing and my art.

Part Four
The Absence of Organized Sound is not Always a Good Thing

Before the reader gets all soft and gooey about the glories of non-organized sound, stop and think. Are there not times when refraining from making organized sound in the form of speech is fatal. A quick "watch out" could save a life. Calling out a friend's name when they are looking for you is a good call.

Then there are other times, when organized sound is crucial. When bigots blast their stuff, to refrain from making a noise. This just empowers the bullies. You have the power to do this. As a matter of fact, doing an extended 4:33 is what helped the Nazis gain power. Zipped lips have sunk ships. Courage is the better part of valor. You the reader have the right and duty to change the things you cannot accept. You have the right and duty to remain vocal. You have the right and duty to think. As George Clinton would say "Think it ain't illegal yet"

On these last few pages, I have put an image or two. Now that you have read what I have to say, you are free to add your own bit of D/G/S/SBW

Thanks Again

Alan Barysh

The Soul Journey with Sarah Moussa

Yesterday at 3:11 AM   ·

If you're exhausted, rest.

If you don't feel like starting a new project, don't.

If you don't feel the urge to make something new, just rest in the beauty of the old, the familiar, the known.

If you don't feel like talking, stay silent.

If you're fed up with the news, turn it off.

If you want to postpone something until tomorrow, do it.

If you want to do nothing, let yourself do nothing today.

Feel the fullness of the emptiness, the vastness of the silence, the sheer life in your unproductive moments.

Time does not always need to be filled.

You are enough, simply in your being.

--Jeff Foster

On The 110ᵗʰ Anniversary Of The Composer John Cage

"If you want to fly, you must give up walking"

John Cage

"I am not scared of new ideas-it's the old ones that scare me"

John Cage

"There is no such thing as silene-It's only the absence of organized sound"

John Cage

Today is the birthday of perhaps one of the most influential abet controversial composers of the last century. Not only did his compositions spark quite a bit of controversy-but they also inspired other musicians and composers. Sadly, all the musical parvenu and yokels of the world can say is something like this. (provided they knew who **John Cage** was) "All he did was walk up to a piano and stare at it! That's not music. And to a neophyte a person who as the composer **Edgar Varese** said: "listen to music with their memories only" (From a letter written to this author) The composition these blunderbusses are talking about is **4:33** where the audience is forced to listen to whatever ambient sounds the venue has. Ideally experiencing this performance would have the astute listener begin to get a grip and realize that life is full of sounds. All we have to do is listen.

And to a lot of composers and musicians' credit, they did. For example, the saxophonist and composer **Anthony Braxton** recorded a piece called **For John Cage** on his album **For Alto**. The multi-cultural classical composer **Lamont Young** was inspired by **John Cage** When the **Beatle, John Lennon** was living across the hall from **John Cage** the story goes that it was **John Cage** that wrote **Revolution Number Nine** (After listening to **The Williams Mix or Some Cartridge Music by John Cage** this will prove what this listener is talking about) Note while **John Lennon** was a next- door neighbor to **John Cage** the composer gave the **Beatle** access to his telephone because **John Lennon** rightly thought his phone was tapped.

With these things in mind let us now reevaluate **4:33. After the Internationale 4:33 is the most revolutionary composition of this or any century** Why does this author say this? Simply, **The Internationale Says "No more traditions chains shall bind us"** and **John Cage** broke the chains of music and it allowed silence to be included in the composition. It allowed composers and musicians to create space in their music. Just listen to the composer /pianist **Keith Jarrett** and you should understand this. This becomes quite clear when **Keith Jarrett** plucks the piano strings on all recorded versions of **Forrest Flower** or any solo piano concert recordings. The same **John Cage** influences can also be seen in the recordings of the composer-pianist **Bill Evans** or composer-multi-instrumentalist **Jimmy Giuffre.**

Not only that, but **John Cage** took A. A, C. M (African American Classical Music as an influence. The **Prepared Piano** that **John Cage** used harkened back to the early days of A.A.C.M when the Boogie Woogie pianists would put thumb-tacks on the mallets that struck the piano keys.

This was called the **Thumb Tack Piano**. Doing this gives the piano a sound like a funky harpsichord.

There's a whole lot more this author could say about this. In his book **On Silence And Other Sounds and in On Time And Space And The Righteous Task of Goofing Off,** this writer goes into more detail. And this author will go into even more detail in his forthcoming work the expanded version of **On Silence and Other Non-Sounds** which like the other books will be published by Amazon.com

Re posted from The Alan Barysh Facebook Page Of Amazing Stuff

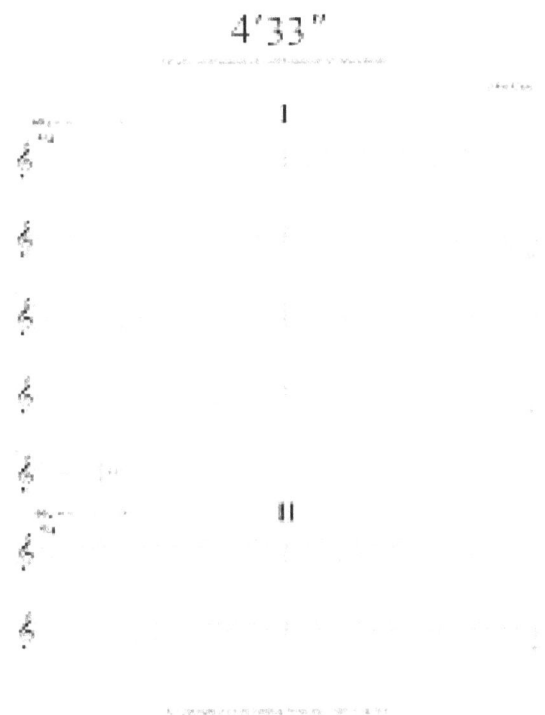

Cage — mon Dieu Adore
mondieu.nu

Tommaso Valletti on Twitter: "4'33" ("four thirty-three") is a 3-movement work by John Cage. Written in 1952 for any instrument or combination of instruments: performer(s) should NOT play their instrument(s) during the

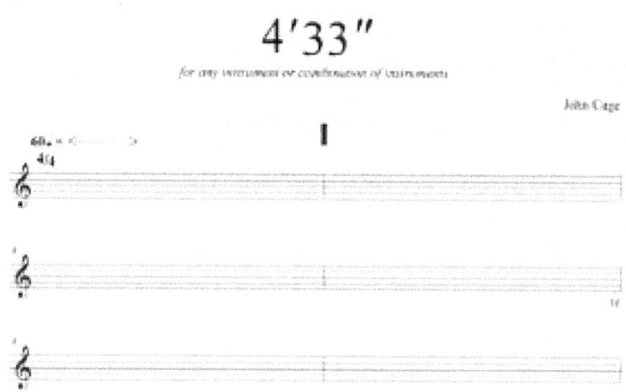

Tommaso Valletti on Twitter: "4'33" ("four thirty-three") is a 3-movement work by John Cage. Written in 1952 for any instrument or combination of instruments: performer(s) should NOT play their instrument(s) during the_twitter.com

12 Variations of John Cage's 4'33 Sheet music for Piano (Solo) | Musescore.com

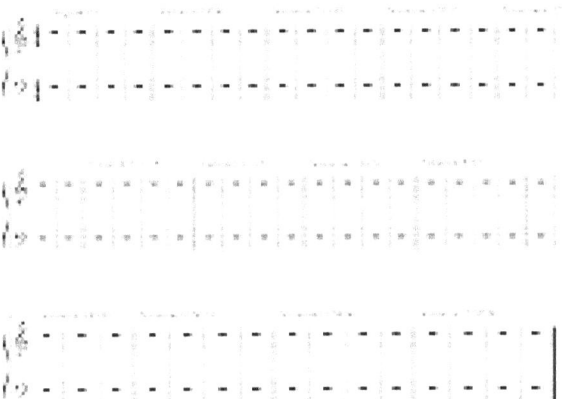

12 Variations of John Cage's 4'33 Sheet music for Piano (Solo) | Musescore.com

musescore.com

For the Record: Documenting Performance

For the Record: Documenting Performance

brown.edu

4'33" – John Cage Sheet music for Piano (Piano Four Hand) |

"Magic doesn't suit everyone only those prepared to take full responsibility for them- selves need apply " Earth Magic Facebook post

4'33" – John Cage Sheet music for Piano (Piano Four Hand) | Musescore.com

musescore.com

4.33 john cage No Minimum Promotional 2021 New Products | Bulk & Wholesale | Free Shipping

Cage in 1988

Born

John Milton Cage Jr.

September 5, 1912

Los Angeles, California, U.S.

Died August 12, 1992 (aged 79)

New York City, U.S.

Alma mater <u>Pomona College</u>Occupation

- Composer
- <u>music theorist</u>
- artist
- philosopher

Spouse

<u>Xenia Andreyevna Kashevaroff</u>

(m. 1935; div. 1945)

4.33 john cage No Minimum Promotional 2021 New Products | Bulk & Wholesale | Free Shipping

f

4'33' (John Cage) » Sheet Music for Ensemble (Score)

4'33' (John Cage) » Sheet Music for Ensemble (Score)
all-sheetmusic.com · In stock

4'33'' - Brass Quintet Arrangement - YouTube

4'33'' - Brass Quintet Arrangement - YouTube

youtube.com

Interlude- Free Form Musings

On The Nature of the Interchangeable Character, Pen Name Generated Character, and any Old Thing That Pops Into My Mind

The Character Groundhog was born a full-grown man on December fifth, 2019. He appeared as a department store Santa picking bits of a toasted coconut doughnut from his teeth. Since then, he has been an underground revolutionary, a homicide cop in a socialist society, a post-communist time traveler, Ulysses, Huckleberry Finn, and now the replacement for Condor in Six Days of the Condor that would slim down to Three Days of the Condor and my even shorter Three Days of The Groundhog. Along the way to this latest reincarnation of Groundhog has popped up as the Deus Ex Machina in this story or that. He was at first a fellow born in the south-then the red diaper baby of an immigrant family from the Soviet Union who came to the United States to do political work and find out where Trotsky was hiding out. So, you see Groundhog had has several personas.

To my knowledge, this is the first time, the character with a name has actually evolved into a character with many personas. In effect, I have created the first character/actor. This character or alter-ego of mine now goes from one literary endeavor to another-keeping his name but reborn and transformed into another character. With a few taps on my keyboard Groundhog can evolve into any person I wish him to be-except a doomed man. The best part about the multi-character I have created is that I have created this character with the real knowledge that he is many characters at the same time. Not only does Groundhog know with certainty that he is many characters in many stories, but he flaunts this. In his own puckish way, he smiles and quotes the Jazz and Blues saxophonist Gene Dindwitti when he says "My name is Perceval Z Fanawski and I've got a secret" he knows that not even the combined efforts of Bill Cullen, Henry Morgan, Fay Emmerson, and Jane Meadows could unravel the secret(s) he knows.

Now I must pause here and tell you, dear readers, who Gene Dindwitti was and how this Perceval Z Fanawski thing began. At one point in his musical career, Gene Dindwitti was a saxophonist in the Paul Butterfield Blues Band. One of the tasks assigned to him was introducing the various members of his band. After letting the audience know who was in the band this Black musician would say "My name is Perceval Z Fanawski, and I've got a secret." You may hear Mr. Dindwitti do this bit on the album The Paul Butterfield Blues Band Live. This recording shows the vast and great potential of what I feel was one of the two great bands Paul Butterfield led.

Now back to our regularly scheduled essay. The idea of a character who also has different personas is like the "real life" actors who portray different people is just a fact of life. So, you have for instance Sir Lawrence Olivier portraying both the sadistic Nazi Josef Mengele in Marathon Man and the Nazi hunter Ezra Liberman in Boys From Brazil and convince the viewing audience he could be both-but at separate times in separate motion pictures. If that is so, then why not create the character/actor who can appear and reappear in books and stories with the same name but perhaps a somewhat different persona? Not only that but perhaps a different persona living in different eras.

With that in mind, why not just alter history too? Why not make people in say pre-civil war America know about things that would be happening later. Why not make Groundhog Finn refer to things that have not happened? Why not give Groundhog a cell phone when cell phones had not been invented? If one can think of a character /actor then why can't one disrupt the real-lifetime events and just have them happen where you want them to happen. After all, this *is* fiction. So, when the Maybe Davies' and The Elana Pretzels' and the Ellen Soup -Kitchens' of the world who do nothing but pretend they can create, come around and point out historical inconstancies in what I have written I can casually point out what I have written has a timeline all of its own and tell wannabe writers or no-writing people they can go pound sand! This is also good for confusing those activists like Richard Ochs who think you can't write a song without footnotes.

Now, let's take this idea one step further in the spirit of the Jackie McLean album One Step Beyond why not write under one or more pen names? And why not create personas around these people you have created to present your writings to the world? After all, if one uses a pen name why not create a character to go with the pen name? then one could honestly say the books written under any other name but yours were indeed character-driven? After all, what's the difference between character-driven written efforts made by you and character-driven efforts made by a pen named character. You see first you create the pen name character-then the character you have invented is free to write from any perspective he or she cares to. And not only that-these characters can write their own autobiographies should they wish to. Why not? As Marion Brown would say. And the best part about using pen names is you can talk all the smack you want and never get caught. Now, this does not mean advocating any anti-social activities-but you can call the Dali Lama a shmuck and that will be that.

So, you see-the potential exists for character/actors to at the author's discretion develop into literally thousands of different personas with different life stories that all have the same-yes the very same name. Like Brown for example. A friend of mine worked at a sub shop near the CIA Headquarters in Langley, Virginia. He said that all of the employees who would call his shop for food pick-ups used the same last name, Brown. This meant that the sub shop had to give each brown a number to keep these orders straight. The author who creates the character /actor does not have to go as far as give numbers like the CIA or Nation of Islam gave to early members of their group. (I E Gerald 23 X because before Gerald 23 X was Gerald 23 X there were 22 other Gerald X's)

With this in mind let me put it to all potential writers. The possibilities of both using the character/actor and adjusting and manipulating historic events to suit your needs in fiction can only lead to the birth of a type of fiction the world has never seen.

⬜⬜⬜⬜⬜⬜⬜

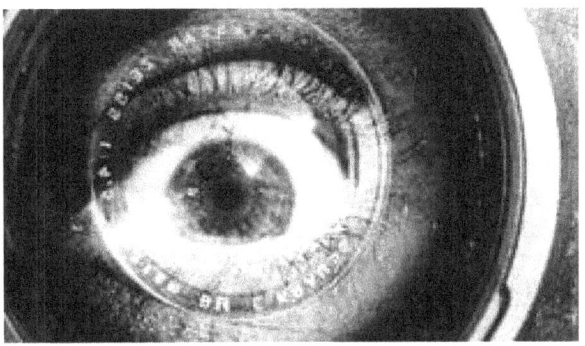

1928) — The Movie Database (TMDB ...
themoviedb.org

This
should
keep
you confused!

This
should
keep
you confused!

Two Essays

On Jigsaw Writing, Collage Writing, The Importance of Listing to What
You Will Write, As Well As Other Topics
By
Alan Barysh
These Words Are Dedicated To
Jean Luc-Goddard

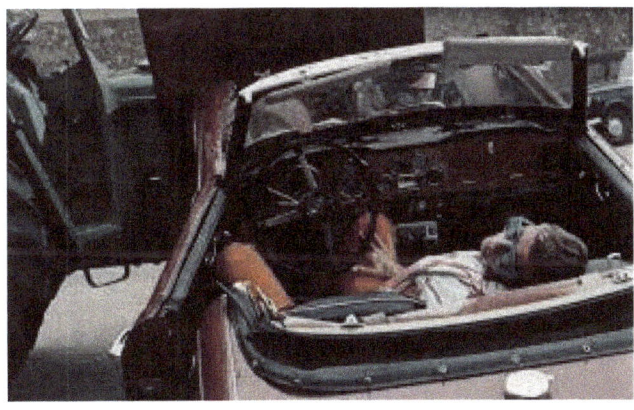

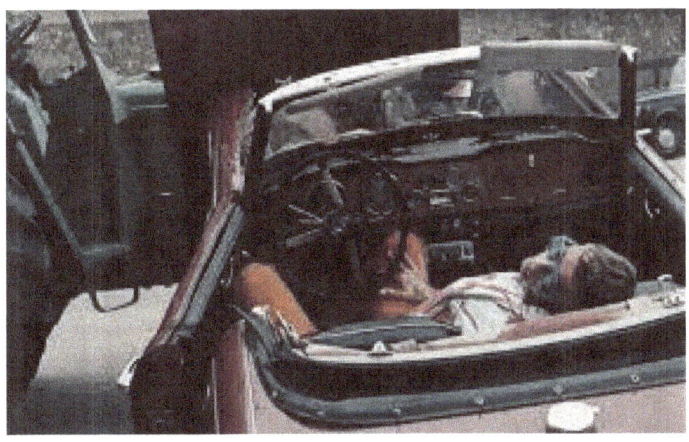

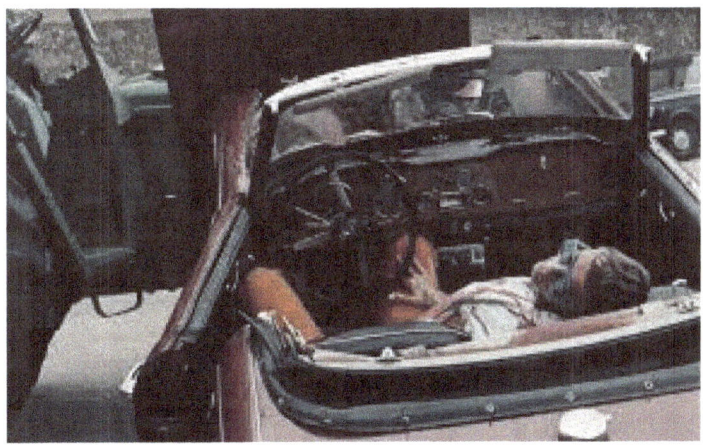

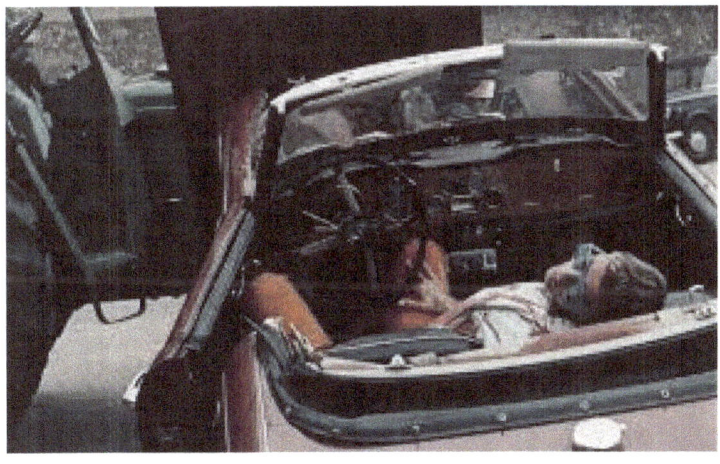

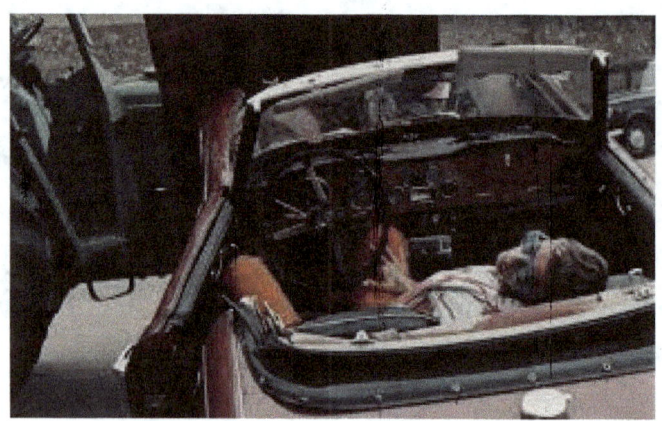

Interlude Within an Interlude
For Jean Luc-Goddard

Jean-Luc Godard

Godard in 1968

On September 13th of this year, Jean Luc-Goddard a giant in the film-making community died by legally-assisted -suicide. For revolutionary-minded people the whole world over, this was a sad day.

This brief bit of homage is not intended for one of the innovative, and provocative filmmakers of the last and this century. It was not just the amazing video effects that made Jean Luc-Goddard such a great artist in the film. Along with the often quite shocking and very often disturbing visuals in the films of Jean Luc-Goddard, there was a very powerful revolutionary message that had its inspiration in the events in China during The Great Proletarian Cultural Revolution. While the "official left" upholds the militant-but-nevertheless non-revolutionary revolution "strike movies" like Norma Rae, Harlan County USA, and the perennial Salt of The Earth that gives the viewers a seriously distorted view of the importance of the labor struggles, the film Tout VA Bien-Jean Luc -Goddard created a movie about a wildcat strike in a sausage factory-where the workers have to go up against both the company *and* the union. This film has some pointed scenes where the union leaders bemoan the fact that this strike is unsanctioned and could upset the time set aside by the union and management for a symbolic strike. When one sees activists who quote Mao ad compare this to Norma Rae where a sorrowful looking Sally Fields is seen holding up a sign that says "union" or Salt of The Earth where the viewer is given the false illusion that after the strike in this copper mine was wone-everything was peachy keen, when in fact the company went out hell bent for leather to nullify this small victory, Tout VA Bien lays bare the philosophical poverty of the trade union ideology. And the sad part about these three movies is the fact that in spite of the rag-rah let's go union-these three films, the cold truth is that whatever concessions that these companies doled out with an eyedropper were snatched back by a steam shovel. It is even sadder to think that these films were made by people who called themselves either communists or socialists.

In contrast to the aforementioned films-Jean, Luc-Goddard made films that supported the struggles in China- and lambasted Soviet-Social Imperialism. In his film Le Chinois there is a puppet show scene where a character that is supposed to be portraying the people of Vietnam call upon the Soviet revisionists to help them. They don't. So, the character portraying the Vietnamese calls on the Chinese. The puppet portraying the Chinese drops a big copy of Quotations From Chairman Mao down to the character portraying the Vietnamese, who then transforms this book into a gun that shoots down toy helicopters, and a puppet looking like Lyndon Johnson comes out waving a white flag.

This is just a sample of the revolutionary films Jean Luc-GOddard made. In See You, At Mao (British Sounds) there's an opening scene where a narrator reads some writings by Karl Marx as the camera shows us an assembly line. In the next, the camera focuses on a naked woman's torso as a female narrator talks about the oppression of women. (This writer found it quite difficult to watch this scene and had to fast forward it) in other films, Goddard talks about the4 role of revisionism in the news, the anti-Vietnam war struggles in the United States, the Chicago Conspiracy trials, and other topics. His iconic film Weekend shows a futuristic society going back to primitive barbarism. On one side you have a class of back-strobing hedonists living in luxury while roving bands of anarchist-cannibals terrorize innocent people and each other using that tired old ends justify the means excuse. The only two good people are the two revolutionary nationalists who haul garbage and a farmer who has his tractor ruined in an accident with a well-to-do young man driving some kind of sports car.

Sadly, this author does not have a lot of knowledge about all the works of Jean Luc-Goddard. However, it would be good if others would dialogue about this and add their viewpoints.

Alan Barysh

Interlude to Interlude

Continued

VIDEO HOMAGE TO JEAN-LUC GODDARD
IN THE STYLE OF WEEKEND

directed by Jean-Luc Godard ...

Jean Luc Godard - #GolfClub

"Give people what they need, food, medicine, clean air, pure water, trees and grass, pleasant homes to live in, some hours of work, more hours of leisure. Don't ask who deserves it. Every human being deserves it" Howard Zinn

letterboxd.com

British Sounds • Senses of Cinema
sensesofcinema.com

Dziga Vertov Group on Notebook ...
mubi.com

CLOSE-UP | British Sounds

closeupfilmcentre.com

Jean-Luc Godard: British Sounds (1970 ...

retentionalfinitude.blogspot.com

British Sounds

filmlinc.org

Sympathy for the Devil ...

popoptiq.com

Amazon.com: British Sounds (See You at ...
amazon.com

British Sounds + Pravda | Metrograph
metrograph.com

British Sounds and Echoes | marckarlin
spiritofmarckarlin.com

British Sounds (1970) – MUBI
mubi.com

Jean-Luc Godard ...
amazon.com

lights in the dusk: British Sounds
lightsinthedusk.blogspot.com

British Sounds + Pravda | Metrograph

metrograph.com

British Sounds (1970) Dvdrip [568MB ...

worldscinema.org

Lotte in Italia (1971) - IMDb
imdb.com

See You at Mao (1970) - IMDb
imdb.com

British Sounds Blu-ray

blu-ray.com

lights in the dusk: British Sounds

lightsinthedusk.blogspot.com

Jean Luc Godard - #GolfClub

"Give people what they need, food, medicine, clean air, pure water, trees and grass, pleasant homes to live in, some hours of work, more hours of leisure. Don't ask who deserves it. Every human being deserves it" Howard Zinn

Jean-Luc Godard + Jean-Pierre Gorin ...

arrowvideo.com

Jean-Luc Godard and the Dziga Vertov ...
stagebuddy.com

Only the Cinema: British Sounds
seul-le-cinema.blogspot.com

British Sounds (1970) – MUBI

mubi.com

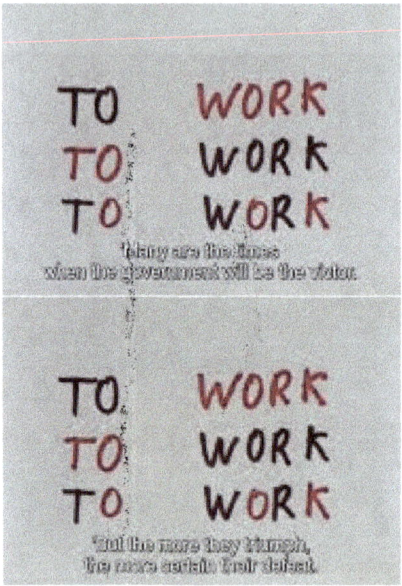

British Sounds Jean-Luc Godard ...

twitter.com

British Sounds (See you at Mao) on iTunes

itunes.apple.com

films that influenced Jean-Luc Godard ...

bfi.org.uk

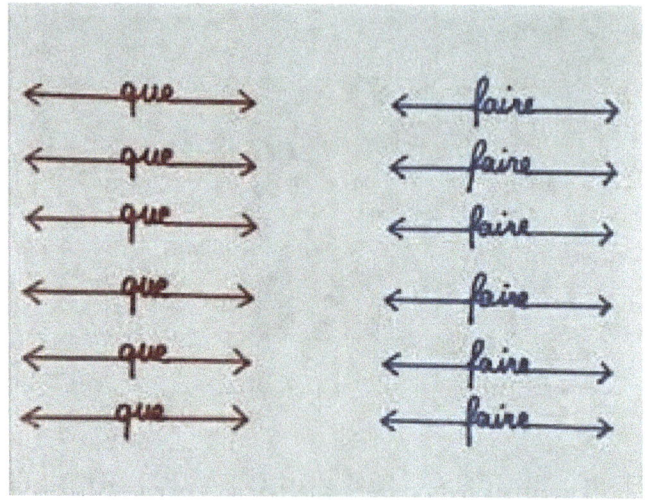

Jean-Luc Godard | What is to be done ...

my-blackout.com

British sounds | Tumblr

tumblr.com

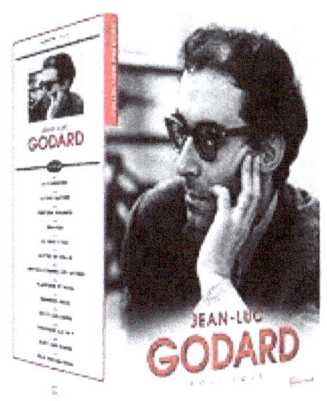

Jean-Luc Godard Collection (13 Films ...

amazon.com

The man is reading Quotations From Chairman Mao

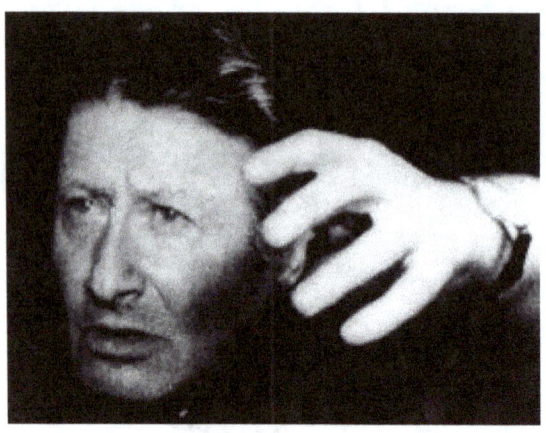

Jean-Luc Godard and Jean-Pierre Gorin's ...

lwlies.com

Jean-Luc Godard + Jean-Pierre Gorin ...

wearecult.rocks

Jean-Luc Godard et Jean-Henri Roger ...

shangols.canalblog.com

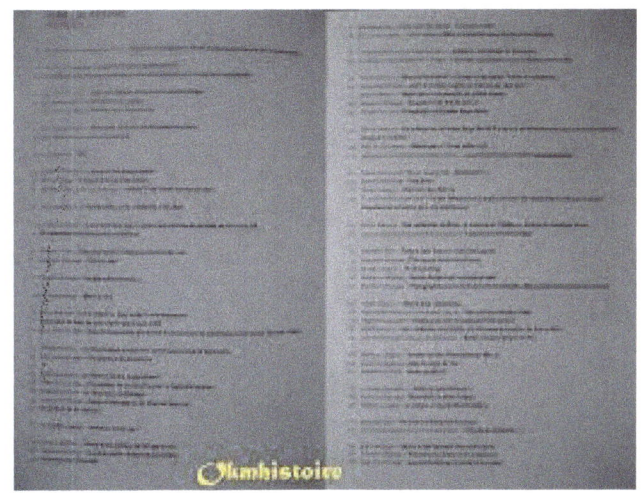

Jean-Luc Godard : Documents ------- + 1 ...

abebooks.com

Jean-Luc Godard + Jean-Pierre Gorin ...

culturedvultures.com

HOME, Manchester – Uprising: Spirit of '68

spiritof68.org.uk

Objective Engagement and Engaged Cinema ...

e-flux.com

Jean-Luc Godard – The Spirit of the Forms

filmlinc.org

Jean-Luc Godard + Jean-Pierre Gorin ...

fetch.fm

Jean-Luc Godard presented with the 2019 ...

faroutmagazine.co.uk

Anne-Marie Miéville's cinema of ...

bfi.org.uk

18. To carry out 1 is to describe the wretchedness of the world.

19. To carry out 2 is to show the people in struggle.

20. To carry out 3 is to destroy 1 with the weapons of criticism and self-criticism.

21. To carry out 1 is to give a complete view of events in the name of truth in itself.

22. To carry out 2 is even to fabricate over-complete images of the world in the name of relative truth.

23. To carry out 1 is to say how things are real. (Brecht).

24. To carry out 2 is to say how things really are. (Brecht).

25. To carry out 2 is to edit a film before shooting it, to make it during filming and to make it after the filming. (Dziga Vertov).

26. To carry out 1 is to distribute a film before producing it.

27. To carry out 2 is to produce a film before distributing it, to learn to produce it following the principle that it is production which commands distribution, it is politics which commands economy.

28. To carry out 1 is to film students who write: Unity – Students – Workers.

29. To carry out 2 is to know that unity is a struggle of opposites (Lenin), to know that the two are in one.

30. To carry out 2 is to study the contradictions between the classes with images and sound.

31. To carry out 2 is to study the contradictions between the relationships of production and the productive forces.

32. To carry out 2 is to learn where one is at, and where one has come from, to know one's place in the process of production in order then to change it.

33. To carry out 2 is to know the history of revolutionary struggles and to be determined by them.

34. To carry out 2 is to produce scientific knowledge of revolutionary struggles and of their history.

35. To carry out 2 is to know that film making is a secondary activity, a small screw in the revolution.

36. To carry out 2 is to use images and sounds as teeth and lips to bite with.

37. To carry out 1 is only to open the eyes and the ears.

38. To carry out 2 is to read the reports of comrade Kiang Tsing.

39. To carry out 2 is to be militant.

JEAN-LUC GODARD January 1970

Translated by Mo Teitelbaum

Jean-Luc Godard | What is to be done ...

my-blackout.com

British sounds by J-L-Godard on Vimeo

vimeo.com

Jean-Luc Godard - Wikipedia

en.wikipedia.org

British Sounds (1970) Dvdrip [2,18GB ...

worldscinema.org

Amazon.com: British Sounds (See You at ...

amazon.com

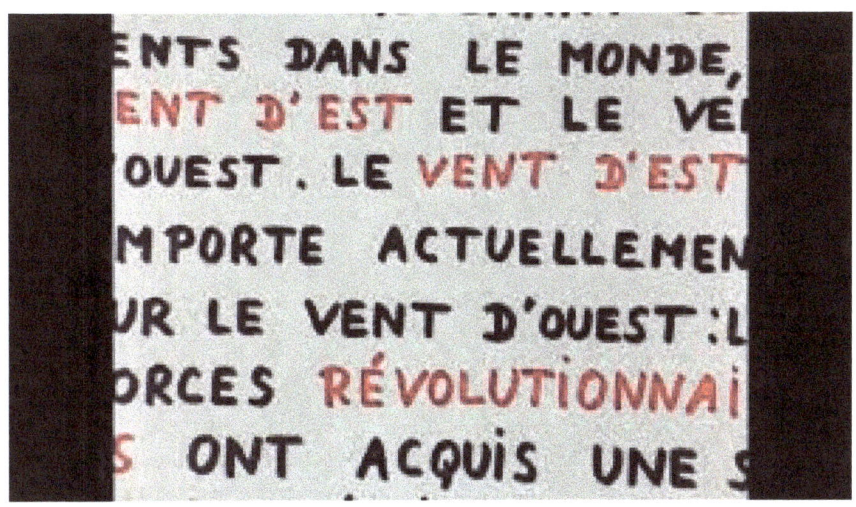

Jean-Luc Godard + Jean-Pierre Gorin ...

10kbullets.com

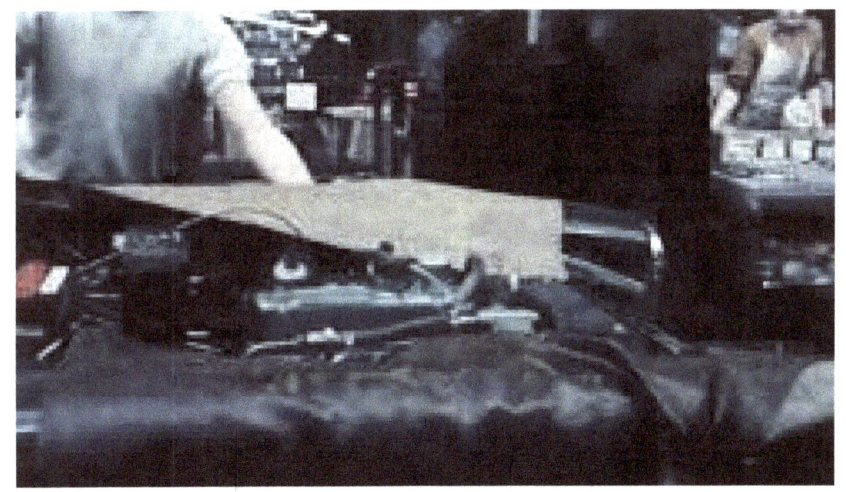

Jean-Luc Godard / British Sounds 英倫之 ...

youtube.com

see you at Mao | Tumblr

tumblr.com

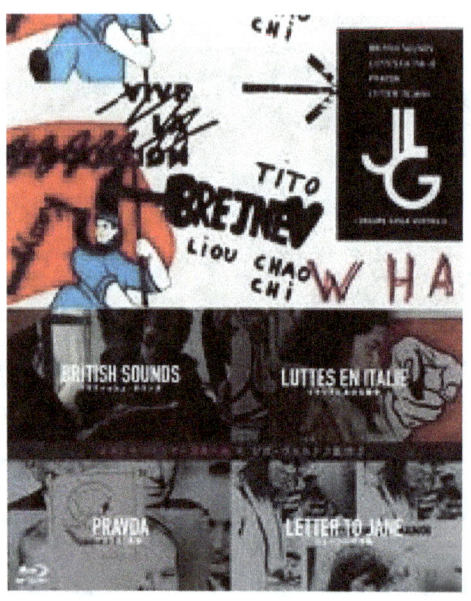

Jean-Luc Godard + The Dziga Vertov ...

blu-ray.com

Struggle in Italy | Metrograph

metrograph.com

Sympathy for the Devil ...

popoptiq.com

The Image Book, Cannes 2018, review ...

independent.co.uk

British Sounds (1970) – MUBI

mubi.com

Jean-Luc Godard | What is to be done ...
my-blackout.com

Jean-Luc Godard | Biography, Movie ...
allmovie.com

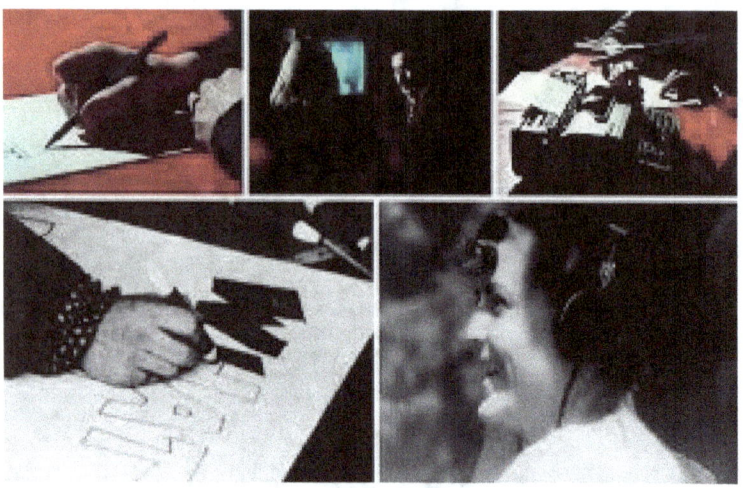

Paradoxes of the Nouvelle Vague

ocec.eu

You say US, I say Mao | Robert Bickers

robertbickers.net

Talk: Albertine Fox on Jean-Luc Godard ...

itunes.apple.com

Three new Blu-ray & DVD releases from ...

cineoutsider.com

BIG SCREEN SOUTHEND

Did You Know -Jean Luc Godard shot ...

twitter.com

Godard "British Sounds" pt. 1 ...

hutnyk.wordpress.com

Jean-Luc Godard and the Dziga Vertov ...

stagebuddy.com

British Sounds and Echoes | marckarlin

spiritofmarckarlin.com

the Godard experience
carleton.edu

British sounds | Tumblr
tumblr.com

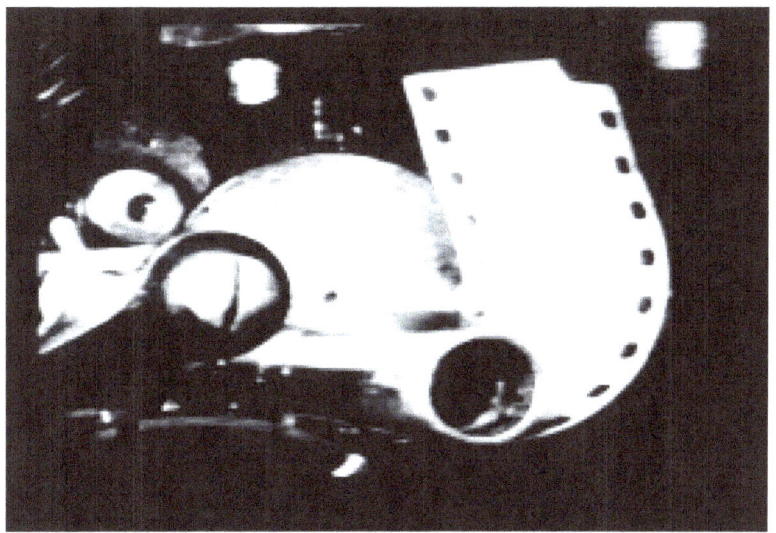

The Image Book' Film Review: Once Again ...

thewrap.com

Jean-Luc Godard + Jean-Pierre Gorin ...

wearecult.rocks

What is to be done?

1. We must make political films.

2. We must make films politically.

3. 1 and 2 are antagonistic to each other and belong to two opposing conceptions of the world.

4. 1 belongs to the idealistic and metaphysical conception of the world.

5. 2 belongs to the Marxist and dialectical conception of the world.

6. Marxism struggles against idealism and the dialectical against the metaphysical.

7. This struggle is the struggle between the old and the new, between new ideas and old ones.

8. The social existence of men determines their thought.

9. The struggle between the old and the new is the struggle of classes.

10. To carry out 1 is to remain a being of the bourgeois class.

11. To carry out 2 is to take up a proletarian class position.

12. To carry out 1 is to make description of situations.

13. To carry out 2 is to make concrete analysis of a concrete situation.

14. To carry out 1 is to make BRITISH SOUNDS.

15. To carry out 2 is to struggle for the showing of BRITISH SOUNDS on English television.

16. To carry out 1 is to understand the laws of the objective world in order to explain that world.

17. To carry out 2 is to understand the laws of the objective world in order to actively transform that world.

What is to be done ? | Diagonal Thoughts

diagonalthoughts.com

Jean-Pierre Gorin: Five Films 1968-1971 ...

bestbuy.com

JEAN-LUC GODARD - French New Wave Director

newwavefilm.com

Brother From Another Planet | The Nation

thenation.com

Godard + Gorin Five Films 1968 - 1971 ...

thenerdmentality.com

British Sounds (1970) Dvdrip [568MB ...

worldscinema.org

The Image Book Trailer: Jean-Luc Godard ...

indiewire.com

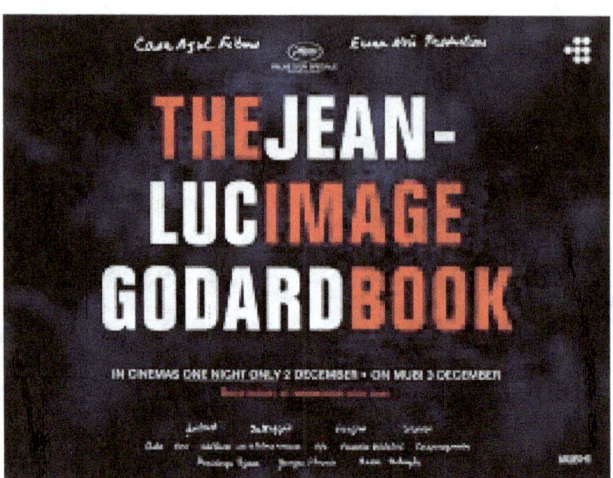

Jean-Luc Godard's 'The Image Book ...

thehollywoodnews.com

British Sounds • Senses of Cinema

sensesofcinema.com

DVDCANFLY

dvdcanfly.com

Godard + Gorin Five Films 1968 - 1971 ...

thenerdmentality.com

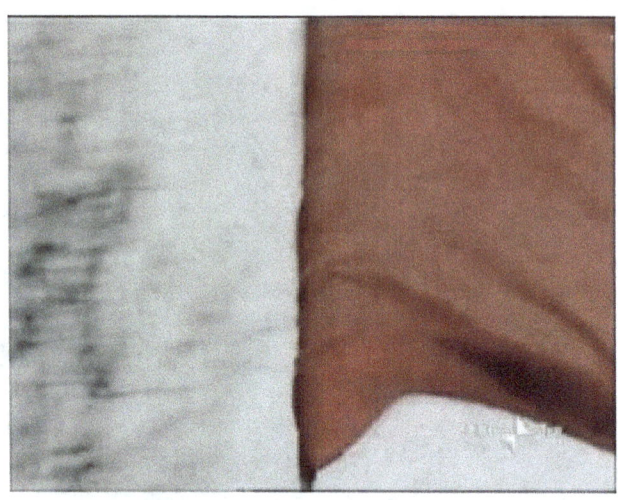

Avital Ronell | FNA Presence Documents

presencedocuments.com

Jean-Luc Godard + Jean-Pierre Gorin ...

blu-ray.com

Anne-Marie Miéville's cinema of ...

bfi.org.uk

Jean-Luc Godard + Jean-Pierre Gorin ...

fetch.fm

Jean-Luc Godard + Jean-Pierre Gorin ...

arrowfilms.com

Tout va Bien | Jean-Luc Godard & Jean ...

inreviewonline.com

See You at Mao (1970) - IMDb

imdb.com

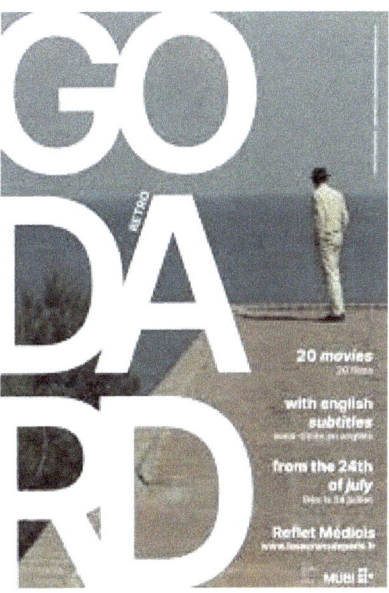

Letters to Jane + British Sounds ...

lesecransdeparis.fr

Jean-Luc Godard nostalgia: is it time ...

theguardian.com

Hell Hath ·No Fury ...

concordia.ca

Jean-Luc Godard and Jean-Pierre Gorin's ...

lwlies.com

Jean-Luc Godard on the politics of ...

youtube.com

Jean-Luc Godard's Latest Film Pushes ...

hyperallergic.com

2 hours ago

Liberation to nudity': an extract from ...

londonreviewbookshop.co.uk

Jean-Luc Godard + Jean-Pierre Gorin ...

dvdtalk.com

Milano Film Festival ...

milanofilmfestival.it

British sounds | Tumblr

tumblr.com

BREATHLESS 1960 FRENCH Film Movie ...

picclick.ie

Michael Witt on Jean-Luc Godard ...

newwavefilm.com

jeanpierregorin • Browse images about ...

imgrum.pw

Jean-Luc Godard to Adapt 'The Image ...

variety.com

L'évènement Jean-Luc Godard - Centre ...

centrepompidou.fr

Jean-Luc Godard & Jean-Pierre Gorin ...

walmart.com

Alan Michael | Frieze

frieze.com

eMoviePoster.com: 2s064 PIERROT LE FOU ...

auctions.emovieposter.com

In Praise of Godard's "In Praise of Love"

jstor.org

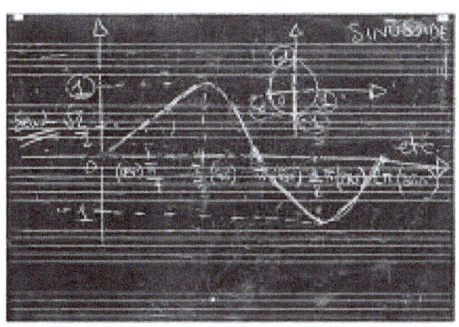

SOUNDWALK COLLECTIVE/Jean Luc Godard ...

phonicarecords.com

PDF) Godard and Sound: Acoustic ...

academia.edu

What is the French New Wave? - Indie ...

indiefilmhustle.com

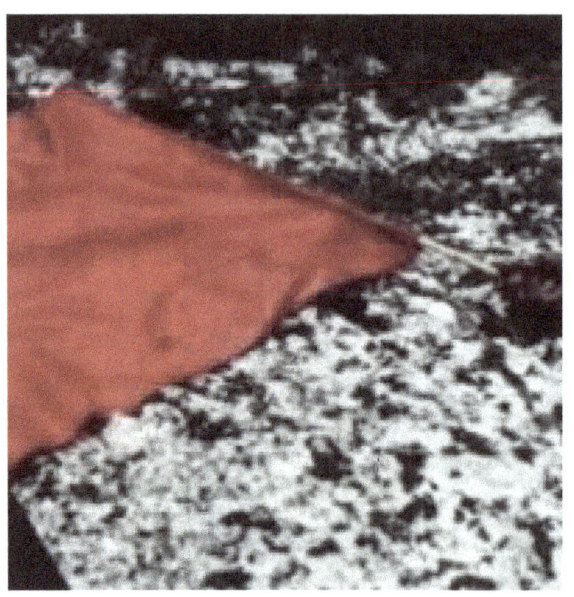

Lisbon & Sinatra Film Festival ...

leffest.com

Jean-Luc Godard Finds Pleasure In ...

vaguevisages.com

3

⑰ Faire 1, c'est comprendre les loi du monde objectif pour expliquer le monde.

⑱ Faire 2, c'est comprendre les loi du monde objectif pour transformer activement le monde.

⑲ Faire 1, c'est décrire la misère du monde.

⑳ Faire 2, c'est montrer le peuple en lutte.

㉑ Faire 2, c'est détruire 1 avec les armes de la critique et de l'auto-critique.

Jean-Luc Godard | What is to be done ...

my-blackout.com

DVDCANFLY

dvdcanfly.com

Film Society of Lincoln Center ...

indiewire.com

Review: Godard + Gorin: Five Films ...

slantmagazine.com

British Sounds (1970) Dvdrip [2,18GB ...

worldscinema.org

Jean-Luc Godard: The Rolling Stone ...

rollingstone.com

directors top 100 films | BFI ...

pinterest.es

Milano Film Festival ...

milanofilmfestival.it

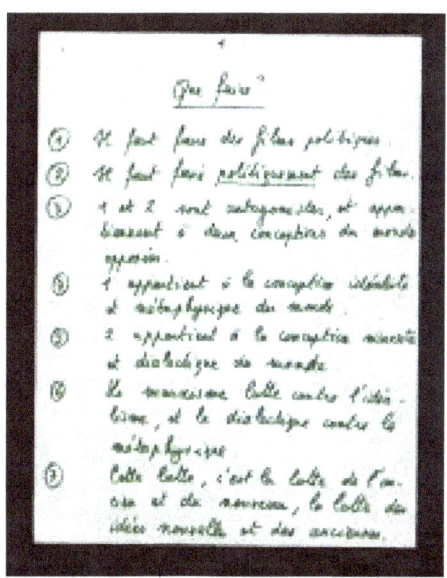

Que faire ? / What is to be done ? - La ...

larevuedesressources.org

Objective Engagement and Engaged Cinema ...

e-flux.com

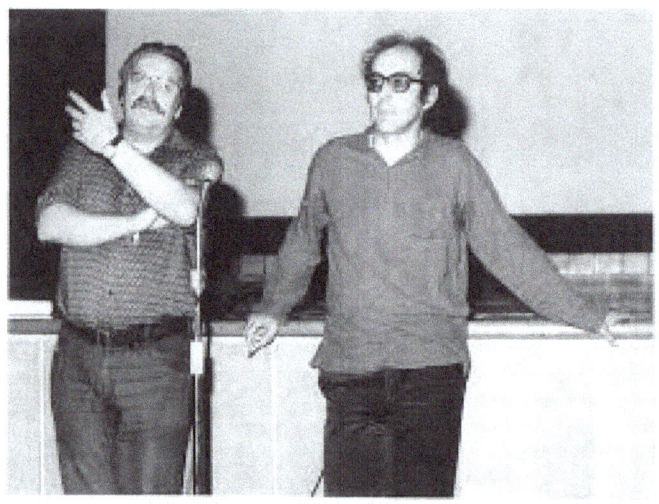

Jean-Luc Godard receives the 2019 FIAF ...

eninarothe.com

Jean Luc Godard - #GolfClub

"Give people what they need, food, medicine, clean air, pure water, trees and grass, pleasant homes to live in, some hours of work, more hours of leisure. Don't ask who deserves it. Every human being deserves it" Howard Zinn

4- 28: Make film politically ...

chtodelat.org

British Sounds (See You at Mao) (1970 ...
rottentomatoes.com

Film - reviewernumber9.simplesite.com
reviewernumber9.simplesite.com

Jean-Luc Godard Solution for Greek Debt ...

altfg.com

Jean-Luc Godard pronounces film dead ...

theguardian.com

Jean-Luc Godard - Director - Films as ...

filmreference.com

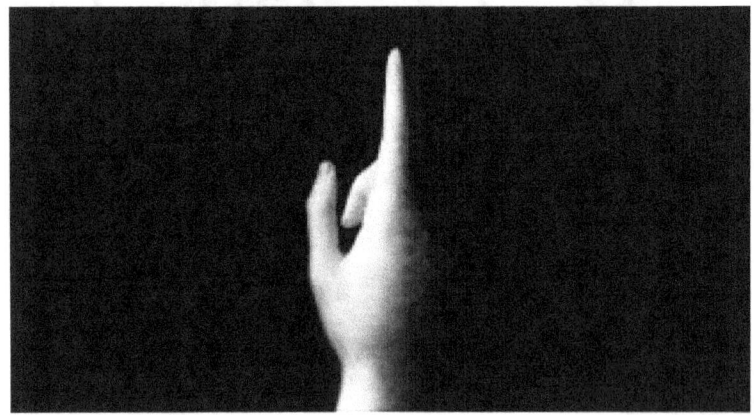

have won Cannes 2018's Palme d'Or ...

bfi.org.uk

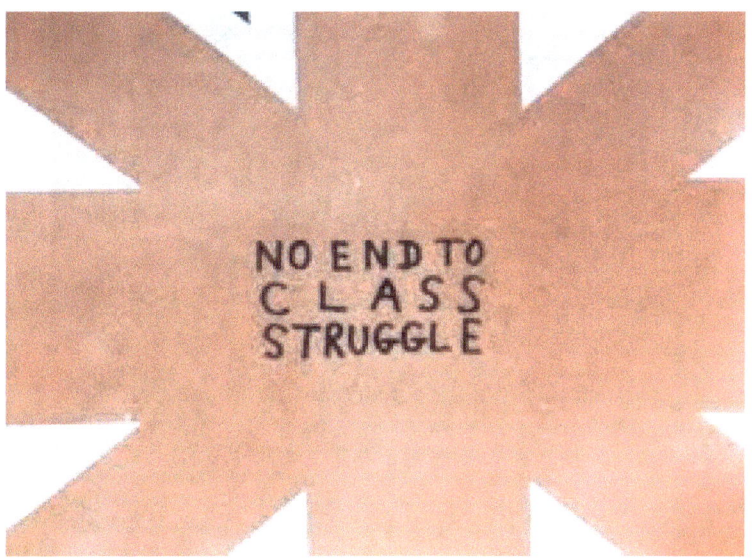

Les Fins de Godard - The Cine-Tourist

thecinetourist.net

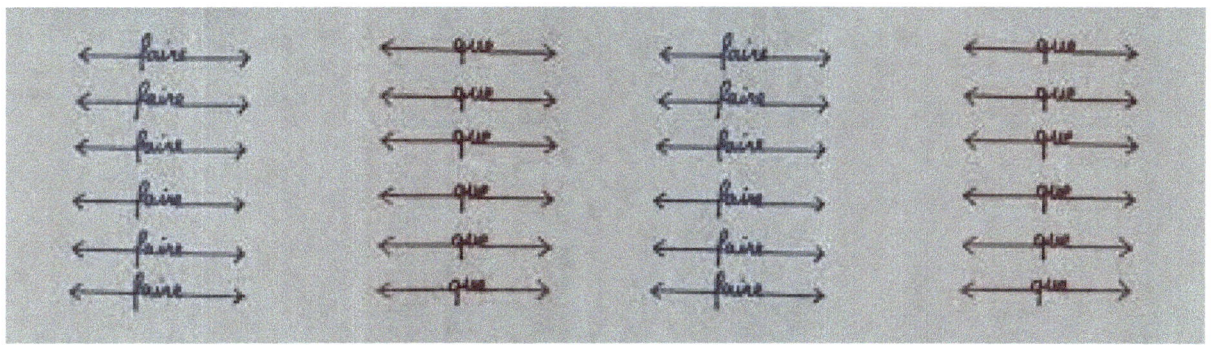

Godard and the Dziga Vertov Group – MUBI

mubi.com

Jean-Luc Godard presented with the 2019 ...
faroutmagazine.co.uk

the Godard experience
carleton.edu

In Praise of Godard's "In Praise of Love"

jstor.org

The invisible woman of French cinema ...

spectator.co.uk

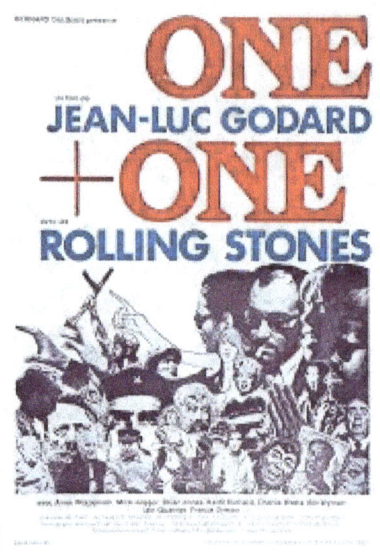

Devil de Jean-Luc Godard ...

en.unifrance.org

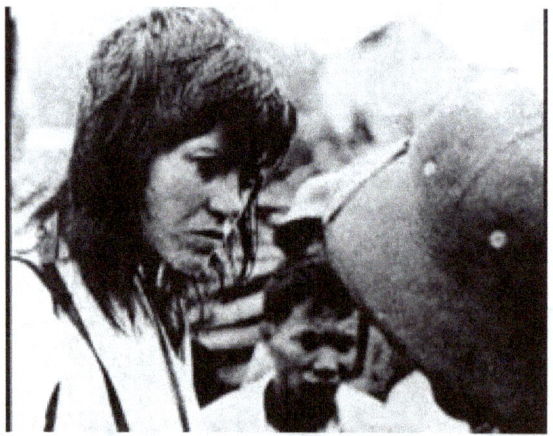

Jean-Luc Godard and Jean-Pierre Gorin's ...

theseventhart.org

Jean-Luc Godard & Jean-Pierre Gorin ...

filmihulluleffakauppa.com

lights in the dusk: British Sounds

lightsinthedusk.blogspot.com

Band of Outsiders (1964) | The ...

criterion.com

British sounds | Tumblr

tumblr.com

Films directed by Jean-Luc Godard ...

letterboxd.com

Godard and the Dziga Vertov Group

donalforeman.com

Jean-Luc Godard + Jean-Pierre Gorin ...
arrowfilms.com

Godard looks through the latest issue of
the Maoist journal La Cause du peuple
at the printer's before it goes on sale,
Paris, November 1970.

Source: AFP. Printed in: Colin MacCabe,
Godard: A Portrait of the Artist at Seventy,
Farrar, Straus and Giroux, New York (2003), page 234

The religion of director Jean-Luc Godard
adherents.com

Jean-Luc Godard + Jean-Pierre Gorin ...

10kbullets.com

The Films of Jean Luc Godard.pdf | Jean ...

scribd.com

Jean-Luc Godard: Voyage(s) en Utopie ...

readthis.wtf

MAY, Quarterly Journal » Sphinx

mayrevue.com

What is to be done ? | Diagonal Thoughts

diagonalthoughts.com

Cinema of Switzerland | The Seventh Art

theseventhart.info

Jean-Luc Godard joins Israel cinema ...

timesofisrael.com

Jean-Luc Godard + Jean-Pierre Gorin ...

dvdtalk.com

Jean-Luc Godard Biography | Fandango

fandango.com

Jean-Luc Godard filmography - Wikipedia

en.wikipedia.org

A Companion to Jean-Luc Godard book ...

sensesofcinema.com

See You at Mao (1970) - IMDb

imdb.com

Jean-Luc Godard, Anne-Marie Miéville ...

moma.org

British Sounds and Echoes | marckarlin

spiritofmarckarlin.com

Jean-Luc Godard Biography – Facts ...
thefamouspeople.com

The Rolling Stones, Jean-Luc Godard ...
discogs.com

Hail Mary - Cohen Film Collection
cohenfilmcollection.net

Sympathy for the Devil ...
popoptiq.com

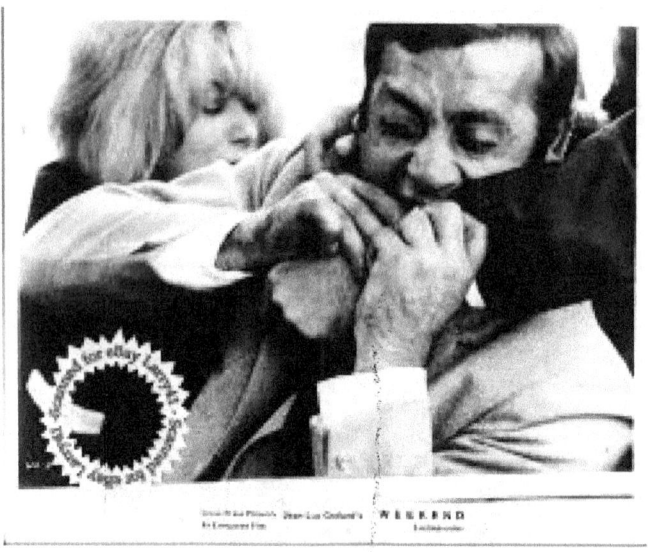

Lot of 4c, Jean-Luc Godard stills ...

worthpoint.com

Jean-Luc Godard's 'Histoire(s) du ...

nytimes.com

Sight & Sound Unveils Its Choices For ...

top10films.co.uk

Jean-Luc Godard's dystopian sci-fi noir ...

nightflight.com

Weekend jean luc godard imdb - The hunt ...

handlaboratory.tk

Jean-Luc Godard honoured with FIAF ...

menafn.com

SOUNDWALK COLLECTIVE/Jean Luc Godard ...
phonicarecords.com

Dozens of Jean-Luc Godard Films Added ...
filmlinc.org

Jean-Luc Godard + Jean-Pierre Gorin ...

fetch.fm

Loneliness of the Long-Distance Runner ...

celluloidwickerman.com

Jean-Luc Godard | What is to be done ...

my-blackout.com

Here and Elsewhere de Jean-Luc Godard ...

en.unifrance.org

Jean-Luc Godard + Jean-Pierre Gorin ...
blu-ray.com

Jean-Luc Godard's 'Militant Filmmaking ...
link.springer.com

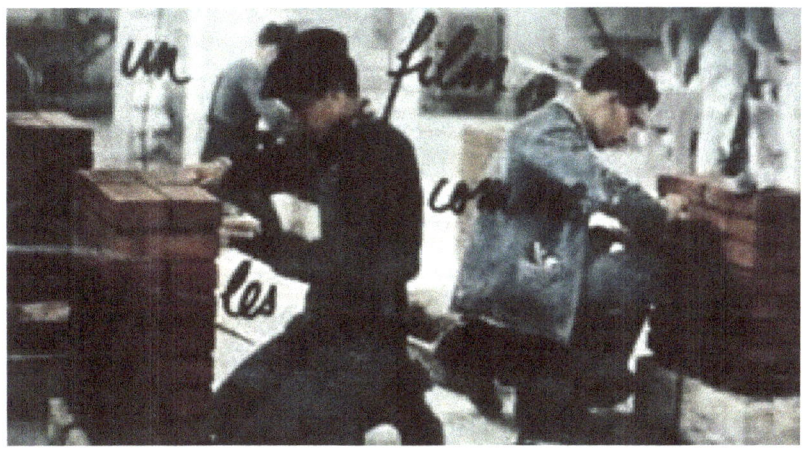

Un Film Comme Les Autres | Metrograph
metrograph.com

jeanpierregorin - Hash Tags - Deskgram
deskgram.net

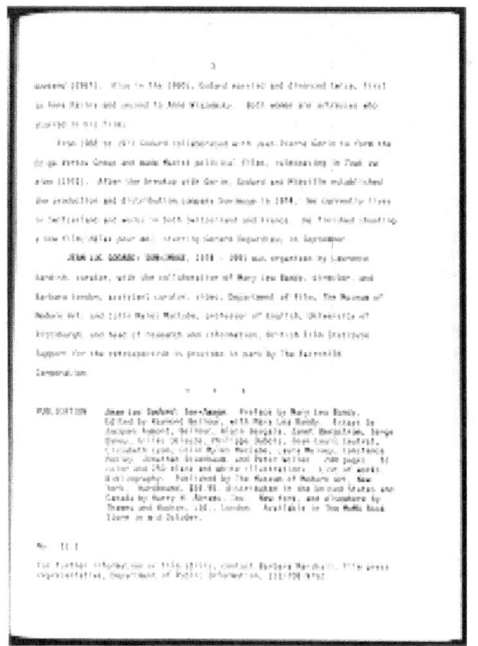

JEAN-LUC GODARD: SON+IMAGE, 1974 - 1991 ...

moma.org

Sessió doble: 'Pravda' i 'British ...

filmoteca.cat

Godard + Gorin Five Films 1968 - 1971 ...

thenerdmentality.com

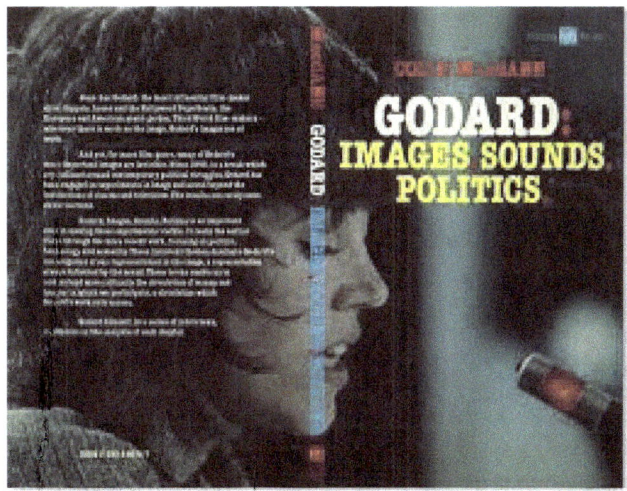

Godard: Images, Sounds, Politics ...

richardhollis.com

Michael Witt on Jean-Luc Godard ...

newwavefilm.com

GODARD + GORIN: FIVE FILMS 1968-1971 ...

youtube.com

The Films of Jean Luc Godard.pdf | Jean ...

scribd.com

ALL-OVER | Magazin für Kunst und ...

allover-magazin.com

Jean-Luc Godard Biography | Fandango

fandango.com

sound editor who helped 'Arrival ...

latimes.com

shooting film for Jean-Luc Godard ...

bfi.org.uk

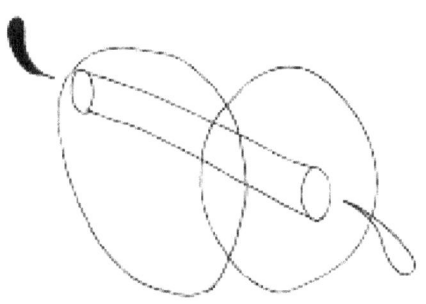

Objective Engagement and Engaged Cinema ...

e-flux.com

MAY, Quarterly Journal » Sphinx

mayrevue.com

In Praise of Godard's "In Praise of Love"

jstor.org

Gift Ideas for Movie Lovers ...

moviebill.com

Jean-Luc Godard's Goodbye to Language ...

chicagoreader.com

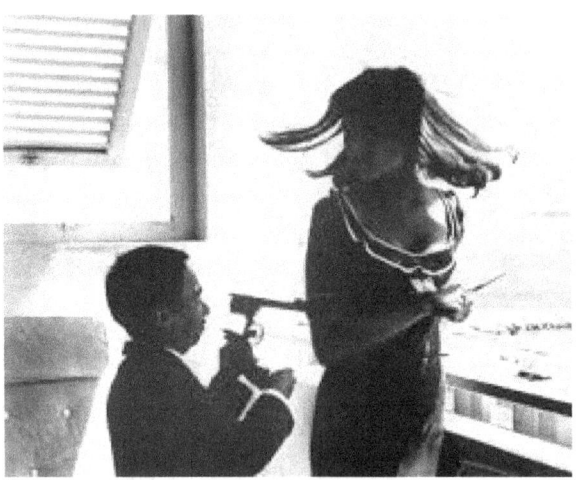

Jean-Luc Godard's Pierrot le fou

assets.cambridge.org

Lot of 4c, Jean-Luc Godard stills ...

worthpoint.com

British Sounds - Pravda - Luttes En ...

fr.shopping.rakuten.com

Four-part documentary series examines ...

thewire.co.uk

100 Documentary Films (Screen Guides ...

bloomsbury.com

Jean-Luc Godard + Jean-Pierre Gorin ...

10kbullets.com

The Importance of Being Perverse ...

jonathanrosenbaum.net

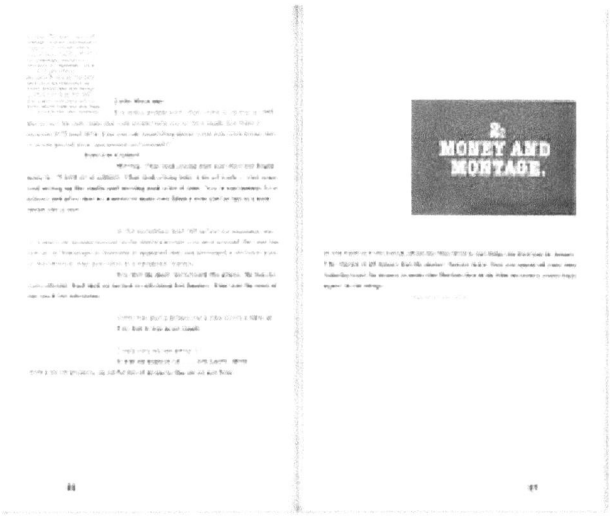

Godard: Images, Sounds, Politics ...

richardhollis.com

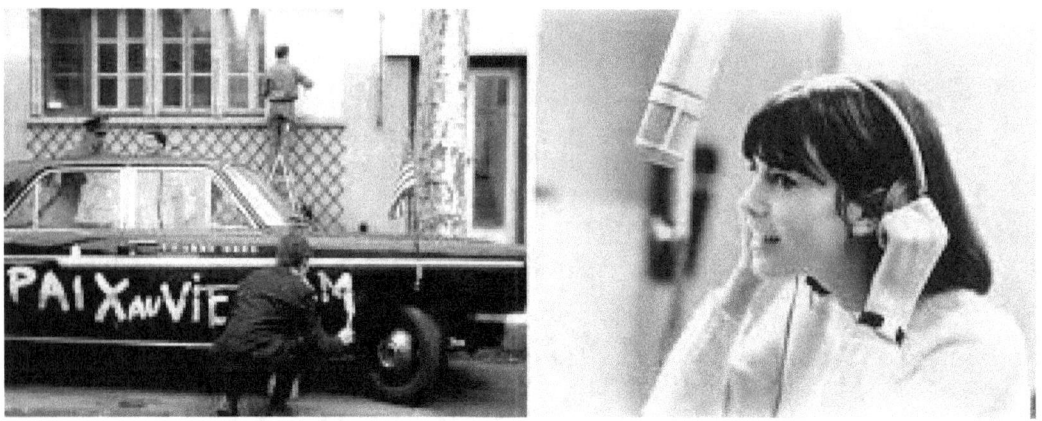

A French Roman. A Story about the ...

ocec.eu

Jean-Luc Godard's dystopian sci-fi noir ...

nightflight.com

Cannes 2018: Lineup Includes New Films ...
variety.com

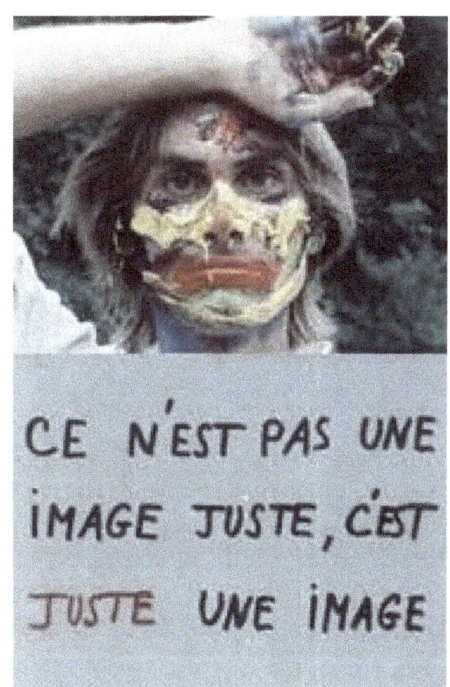

Jean-Luc Godard ...
letterboxd.com

French New Wave: The Influencing of the ...

thefilmstage.com

British Sounds | Não são as Imagens

naosaoasimagens.wordpress.com

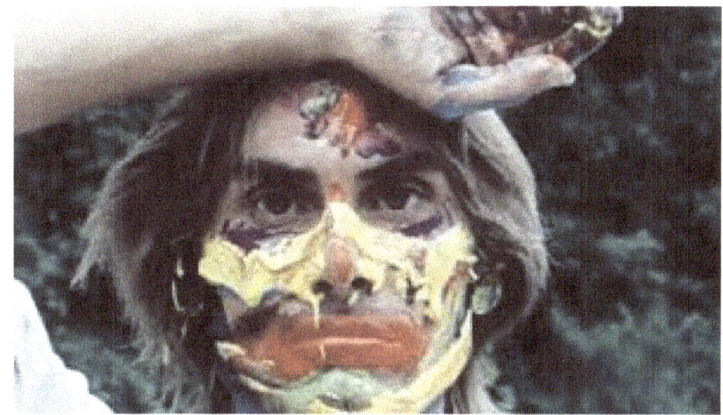

Godard+Gorin: Five Films ...

brooklynrail.org

Michel Hazanavicius on his film ...

theguardian.com

A Companion to Jean-Luc Godard book ...

sensesofcinema.com

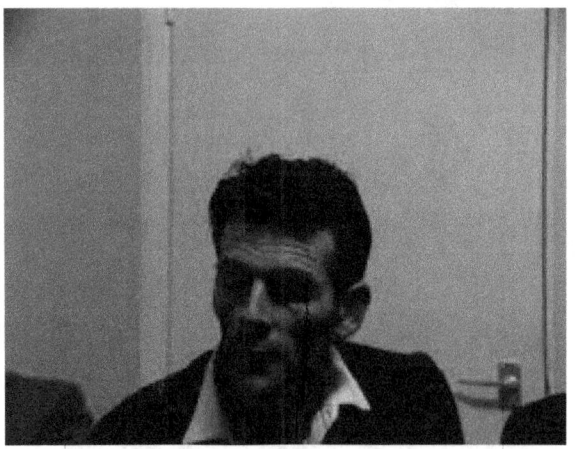

British Sounds (1970) Dvdrip [2,18GB ...

worldscinema.org

British sounds | Tumblr

tumblr.com

For Ever Mozart by Jean-Luc Godard ...

barnesandnoble.com

Michel Legrand: Oscar-winning French ...

independent.co.uk

GODARD + GORIN - FIVE FILMS (1968-1971 ...

framerated.co.uk

The Unforeseen Journey from Jean-Luc ...

cinemasojourns.com

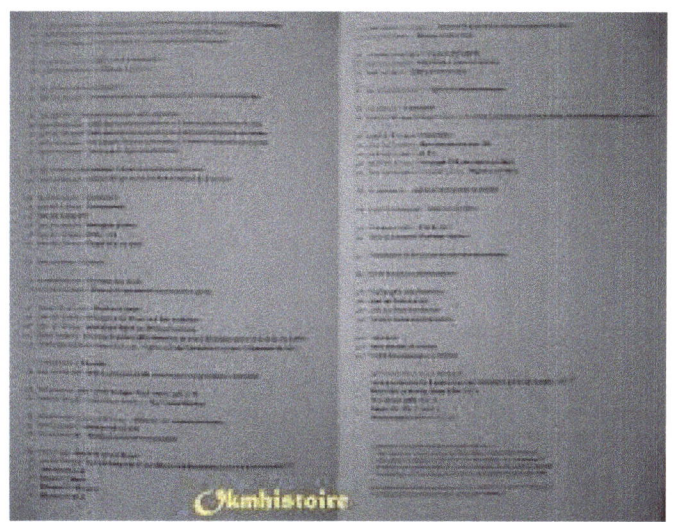

Jean-Luc Godard : Documents ------- + 1 ...

abebooks.com

Jean-Luc Godard receives the 2019 FIAF ...

eninarothe.com

Film posters ...

pinterest.com

sound editor who helped 'Arrival ...

latimes.com

BBC Sound Effects library available to ...

thewire.co.uk

Review: Godard + Gorin: Five Films ...

slantmagazine.com

King Lear (1987 film) - Wikipedia

en.wikipedia.org

donalforeman.com   about films writing links

Godard and the Dziga Vertov Group

donalforeman.com

Jean-Luc Godard: Voyage(s) en Utopie ...

readthis.wtf

Jean-Luc Godard - Best Film Moments

refinery29.com

Sound of Music 1965 British Quad Poster ...

posteritati.com

TSPDT - Jean-Luc Godard

theyshootpictures.com

The Image Book' Film Review: Once Again ...

thewrap.com

Contempt (1963) | The Criterion Collection
criterion.com

Jean-Luc Godard + Jean-Pierre Gorin ...
dvdtalk.com

Capernaum: give children the right to ...

11polaroids.com

What is to be done ? | Diagonal Thoughts

diagonalthoughts.com

the Godard experience

carleton.edu

Jean-Luc Godard's Innovative Filmmaking ...

openculture.com

The Films of Jean Luc Godard.pdf | Jean ...

scribd.com

Jean-Luc Godard - UniFrance

en.unifrance.org

British Sounds and Echoes | marckarlin

spiritofmarckarlin.com

Jean-Luc Godard

newwavefilm.com

Jean-Luc Godard Finds Pleasure In ...

vaguevisages.com

Jean-Luc Godard | Biography, Movie ...

allmovie.com

lights in the dusk: British Sounds

lightsinthedusk.blogspot.com

Jean-Luc Godard's Breathless: The ...

ro.ecu.edu.au

Jean-Luc Godard and Jean-Pierre Gorin's ...

lwlies.com

Sight & Sound: the February 2016 issue ...

bfi.org.uk

Playful and Contemplative: The Sounds ...
fandor.com

Godard + Gorin Five Films 1968 - 1971 ...
thenerdmentality.com

Jean-Luc Godard + Jean-Pierre Gorin ...

arrowfilms.com

See You at Mao (1970) - IMDb

imdb.com

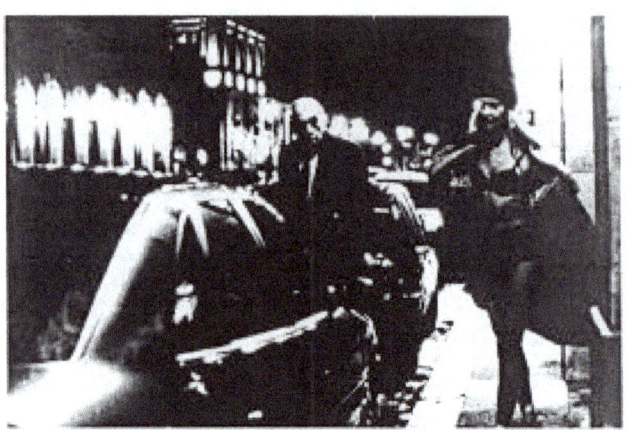

In Praise of Godard's "In Praise of Love"
jstor.org

British Sounds Paul Burron,jean-luc ...
mauronline.it

Hakawati - We Are The Stories We Tell

hakawati.co.uk

Sympathy For The Devil 4K - Film Clip ...

youtube.com

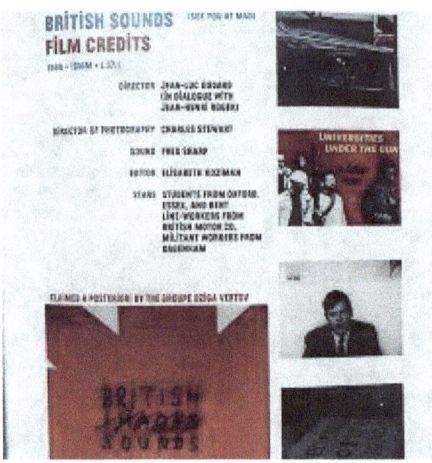

British sounds for all Instagram posts ...
publicinsta.com

The 39 most stylish films of all time ...
gq-magazine.co.uk

Jean-Luc Godard + Jean-Pierre Gorin ...

culturedvultures.com

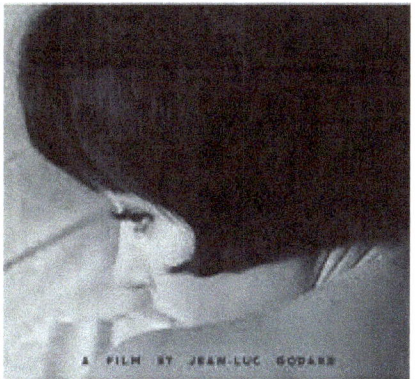

Vivre sa vie Blu-ray review - Part 1 ...

cineoutsider.com

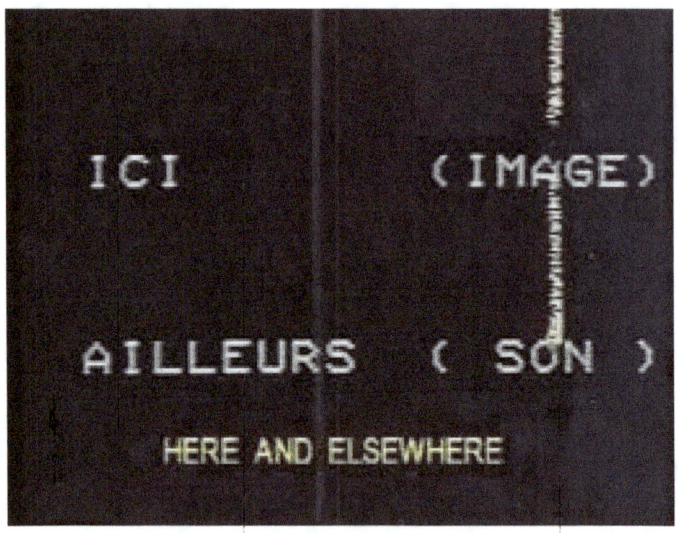

Close-Up on Jean-Luc Godard's "The Rise ...

mubi.com

I do hope by now, that the reader will see what I mean, after reading This series of books. With that in mind, I go on. In my first introduction, I talk about ghost writing/spirit/dream writing. I would like to go into what I mean by dream writing. As anyone who has dreamt knows, aside from being a wish your heart makes, dreams have a logic all their own. So, in dream writing, sometimes the story has a logic all its' own. In one book, the Mish Mosh Zone is called The Mish Mosh Area, in other places, the streets are incorrectly named. In other places the geographical areas do not conform to geographical areas in real life. In short, these volumes are in a word, a fact checkers nightmare. Any factchecker, would have a field day proving the outright inconstancies in what I have indeed written. And much to their chagrin, I would have to say in the words of Ed McMahon : You are correct sir!" And then remind him that in the words of Pea Wee Herman in Pea Wee's Big Adventure: " I meant to do that!"

Part Two
There is Shock Value, and there is Shock Value

After watching a number of Goddard's films, one would obviously see just what I was talking about. For example, I would not tell a member of my family who were conservatives to watch the Goddard Film about Lenin and Rosa Luxembourg without expecting to get into a long drawn- out argument. However, I might suggest that a leftist history major, who fancies themselves to be a hippie or a spiritualist to watch this movie, to show them the sixties were not all about butterflies, flowers, psychedelics, free love, and tie died underwear. I would hope that the modern member of the Rainbow Family, would for a few seconds in their purple hazed foolishness see the clash of forces that shook the world, could not be found in the recordings of hippie bands with white male lead guitarists. I would also show this movie to every Trotskyist , Social Democrat and revisionist I could find, just to show them how *little* effect they had in the sixties. You see, there are times you do not want to shock people, and there are times you don't. And, putting a little shock into a hippie or Social Democrat or any of the respectable left's life is not all that bad. However, there's shock and there's shock. For example, take the shock for shocks' sake of all the slasher films or the early John Watters films. In my opinion they were just gross. And while in some circles, I would be considered to be quite bourgeois and square for saying that, I would reply, that, my personal tastes are such that I can't watch those types of films, but can watch Quinten Tarentino films and not bat an eyelash. I did like Rubber and Cars That eat people. I did not like Pink Flamingos. So, when I talk about wanting to shock people, or give them a jolt, I let the structure of the work do the shocking. And I try to do something that will raise a few eyebrows. For example, I never use profanity or descriptions of sexual activity in these writings. Why you ask. It's simple, I just want to buck the tide of what has become passé in the so-called rebellious art circles. That is why I made two of the central characters The Dietz Brothers devout Christians, with happy home lives. Let Arthur Conan Doyle or Walter Mosley have their heroes with drug habits , or dysfunctional home lives. I prefer the Ellery Queen private investigator in what I write, not what I read. (That is with the exception of Flavia DeLuce and the Number One Ladies Detective Agency)

At this point, I would like to talk a bit about The Dietz Brothers. I got the last name Dietz from looking at a delivery truck from a meat packing company called Dietz and Watson. What better pun. First there was Holmes and Watson, now we have Dietz and Watson. I just dropped the Watson. Benjamin Dietz, because of Big Ben, the clock, that's always on time. William Dietz, because of the phrase "Where there's a WILL, there's a way" In other words as long as Will is on the caser, the case will be solved. I also wanted The Dietz Brothers to have strict standards in the movies that they watched. Ergo I created The Dietz Test. That test rates any film with the slightest bit of offensive language or anything else to be off limits to their viewing. However, with a lot of violence in this series, I chose with one exception or two, not to have them involved in any violent actions. (Even though I do mention that they were in the Military.) Now that I have made that point, I would like to turn my attention to I call The Respectable Rebel, The Faux Rebel, The Real Rebel, The Nihilist/Neoist Rebel and The Church of The Sub -Genius.

There are Rebels, And There are Rebels

Not everyone who calls themselves a "Rebel" is in fact what they are in reality. Let's take a look at the people who are or are not rebels.

1) There's the faux rebel. You in the arts circle know this type. They are usually white males who have either a drinking habit or a drug habit ,or both. They sulk about at their gallery openings, distaining to speak to anyone that cannot advance their futures. They think that exhibiting or reading out is strenuous to their selfish souls. They view themselves as suffering for their art. They never see themselves as a source for joy, inspiration or intellectual stimulation for others. All they think about is themselves. All they think about is themselves, and they hope that all you think about is them. At poetry readings, if there is an open mike after the reading, they leave when they are finished, shepherding their friends and associates with them. This usually includes any sycophantic students in their lit classes hoping their grades will go up, because they are at the readings. These phony rebels avoid being part of any movement for positive change, while this movement is considered a "fringe element". However, once the mainstream of their society embraces the cause, these undercooked phonies rush to the forward lines of struggle, with banners emblazoned with their bold looking profiles on them, acting like they have been there all along as the bark orders to those who have been involved in this struggle for years. If you want examples of faux rebels, the names Anselm Hollo and "Blaster" Al Akerman are perfect examples.

In their heydays I do believe they were both the most obnoxious men I ever met. To his credit, Anselm Hollo did sober up. However, unlike most boozers who try and make good with the people who still have footprints on the tops of their shoes from these fools, Mr. Hollo never did try and make good to anyone in Baltimore, that he offended. And his followers thought the people he hurt, should get over their hurt. Blaster" Al Akerman lived his life as what I would call a drunken sot. He had nothing but contempt for anyone who did not look up to him. Like the late Anselm Hollo, he was known for being a rude heckler. Unlike Anselm Hollo, he was what I would call a gibberish writer. To be quite frank ,nothing he wrote made any sense to me. Then there is the case of Gale Danley. I have seen her do the same piece of "performance art" where she tells people either her mother has *just* died or her daughter has gone missing *at least* four times. *Every* time she has done this, she tells the audience, that these events have *just happened* ! That would mean two thgings.1) Her mom has died and ben resurrected more than once and 2) She needs to buy her daughter a cell [hone with a GPS in it that cannot be turned off, otherwise the audience will see a blubbering poet who has more tears than Niagara Falls has water. Abd to top it off, this woman will leave straight after she is done performing, in order not to talk to anyone that came to the event.

2) The real rebel often works for change for decades. More often than not. They are viewed as a pariah. If they are artists, they are lucky if they can get a place to show their art that isn't the guest space in the loft where they live. If they are writers and are part of a group of

people reading, the person in charge of the readings worries that they might make the people who came to the reading feel nervous. Unless by some odd fluke they do become famous, they will live with the hope that the legacy they leave behind will do right by them.

3) The Nihilist/ Neonist Rebel is a thorn in the side of conventional art. One of the guiding lights is TENTAVITY a CONVIENCE. This man defies all sorts of categories. His associates also do the same. May God have pity on the poor soul should they become victims of his scathing satire. And may the world be amazed at the ensembles he has created, as well as his films and various and sundry contraptions. This goes for all the Neonists in the world today.

4) The nihilists are sort of the same. However, when they are off the mark, they are off the mark.

5) The Church of The SubGenius is a hoot. (That is if they are still around) Take them as seriously as you like, they don't give a hoot one way or another.

Part Three Just Why Are The Enemies In Your Books The But Of Your Anger?

That is quite simple. These groups and ideas represent in my opinion some, but not all of the dregs of society. I will in a few sentences tell you just why they deserve my wrath. I will go group by group and tell you more.

1) Libertarians AKA Zen Anarchists These are a heartless group of vampires only slightly worse than the fascists. I say slightly worse, because they do not (at this point) have any desire to start building concentration camps. From what I know about Libertarians is that they are in my opinion fascists who know nothing about history, but like to get high. I say that they know nothing about history, because when I tell them that they are fascists, they reply that fascists are left wing. They point to the Nazis. They say NAZI is anacronym for National Socialist Workers Party. They do not see the difference between NATIONAL Socialism the wrapping of the word socialism into the folds of National Chauvinism to create something really foul. They also have no knowledge of history. One need only look back at the robber baron era. If this country were ever to fall into their grips anything decent that people fought and died for would be chucked under the juggernaut of the rights of "THE INDIVIDUAL" THE INDIVDIUAL is king. And in the eyes of these parasites, nothing should stand in the way of INDIVIDUAL FREEDOM. If a minimum wage gets in the way of THE INDIVIDUAL employer, the answer to these low lives is simple-abolish the minimum wage. If their employees complain that they

The Big Book About Sounds

cannot survive on the paltry sums of money these INDIVIDUAL bosses dole out the have two replies.1) No one is forcing you to work here-get another job. However, when they say there are fewer and fewer jobs out there these fat cats say 2) Get a second job. Now that's rich. These foul traducers want for nothing have the chutzpah to reduce human beings into talking tools who only live to work, reproduce and work some more. Now when people point the selfish nature of these putrid people, they point out that a minimum wage hurts all workers, *especially* workers of color and women. They use pretzel logic to say that THE INDIVIDUAL boss can hire more workers if they do not have to pay a minimum wage. Well, if that is so, then logically paying workers nothing and herding them into worker Bantustans would really be the answer to their prayers. In this scenario, they wouldn't have to pay their employees anything and they could work them for as long as they like. Other things that would be axed by these articulate hooligans would be affirmative action. I heard on Libertarian/Zen Anarchist say that affirmative action was bad, because and I quote "You can't make someone like you!" Public education would be scrapped, and the burden of bringing up educated children would be foisted on parents who would have no time to raise these children, because they would be at work. What would happen? There would whole generations of people who would only know enough to work reproduce and go to work. The environment would be a mess. With no government regulations every ounce of air would be sucked out of the atmosphere. And life as they know it would end. Along with the decline of civilization would come a rise in drug addiction and prostitution and child prostitution. The logic of these well -suited thugs has been stated in their own press. They say, you should not put any restraints on THE INDIVIDUAL, and if that's what these people want to do, then, they should be allowed to do this safely. They even refuse to call alcoholics or addicts what they are. There is no room in their vocabulary for that. As for prostitutes, the word these garbage bugs call them is "Sex Workers" as if this was a normal job. These pond vermin even like pornography. They say that both pornography and prostitution somehow "empower" those who engage in it! Now I must point out that Zen Anarchists and other forms of anarchists do not have much in common. Anarchists believe in creating a society of free association. They do not have the answers that I have been looking for. Zen Anarchists have the same answers as Libertarians with just a bit of window dressing to make them appear to be different.

CHAPTER FOUR

End of Interlude in the Interlude
We Now Return You To Your Regularly Scheduled Interlude

On Jigsaw Writing

In continuing to be honest with people who read the words that have been put on the pages that have been written by this author, I have to confess, that it gives me a somewhat great feeling of satisfaction when some no-writing no-analytical individual with no sense of amazement with the discovery of things heretofore untried in literature or the arts comes up to me and says they find some of the things that I write to be confusing.

Why is that so? The answer is simple. First of all, it means that what I have written has defied the bounds of both conventional writings of the scholarly type, and hopefully has not pushed the envelope, but shredded the envelope of the state-sanctioned "Avant-Guarde" while shattering, the illusions of the Agit-Prop Crowd.

That being said it is however not intended to shock people, for example, the works of John Watters or Kenneth Anger. My writing just wants to baffle people like the music of John Cage, or Anthony Braxton. And I might add, the films of Jean Luc Goddard.

Let me start at the end of a series of books that I have written. These books were collectively call A Remembrance of Cookies Past (This is a direct double pun on the books written by Marcel Proust called Remembrance of Things Past) The first paragraph of this series of books, has two characters who are department store Santa Clauses eating doughnuts. The book then developed its' own life and spanned what I called a three series collection, much the way a television show would have series one, two, etc. However, in my haste, I did not number them at first on the covers of each volume. Later, I did this. However, when a potential reader goes to purchase these books om Amazon.dot.com to purchase these books, the sheer volume of my output is I am afraid to say rather daunting. Rather than go back to clear things up, I decided to let things stay as they were. That was because I thought that this would force any reader that actually liked what I had written to buy all of my books. Then I thought of the person who enjoys doing jigsaw puzzles/ The jigsaw aficionado has somewhat of an idea about how the puzzle will end. However, once the puzzle pieces are dumped on a table, the completed picture is still unclear.

I reasoned that if this was okay for the average jigsaw person, why not ramp things up for the above-average reader who likes a challenge? I had already started working on what I called scrapbook writing, where I included pictures and asides to the reader, making the book sort of non-linear, so why not do more by not showing the reader just which book follows the next. However, should a major distributor decide that they would publish my works in sequence, I won't compline too much. However, for the time being, I will go with what I have.

The reason is that for too long, the average person has been pandered to in a way that makes the average writer, stay the average writer. Just look at your average grocery store book shelve. I defy you to find anything that is not pablum in print! Listen to your average music station. You will find nothing mind stirring played on the air. Listen to A.M. talk you will find urine disguised as apple juice being foisted upon the people. There you have it. And what makes it worse is that there are a lot of alternative "alternatives" that are not that alternative! For example, take your F.M. Classical/Jazz radio station. Ask yourself why is the Jazz only on at Night? Why don't the so-called "Electronic" music stations play one of the founders of *real* electronic music Edgar Varese on their airwaves? Why are there not more bars and night clubs that cater to music that appeals to lovers of different music? Why are is it that the only choice a lover of *real* experimental music is some dingy bar or a high-priced "festival" where there is not a real variety of music? [5] Why is it that there are no new Jazz groups to carry the torch of The Art Ensemble of Chicago or Albert Ayler

---

[5] A good case in point is the High Zero festival that was or is held in Baltimore. True it is an all-inclusive affair. However, from what little I have seen the music lacks a certain spark. Perhaps it's because the founder of the festival John Berndt likes it that way. I just find it not what I am looking for when I want to be amazed.

when given the chance? Why isn't Archie Shepp performing Portrait of Robert Thompson as a Young Man anymore? Where is Carla Bley? Why don't more people know who Mathew Shipp is? Why has the Frank Zappa legacy been placed in the cubicle labeled rock star and not skilled musician and composer? Where is Laurie Anderson?

In the field of art, where are the Robert Rauschenberg's' The Gasper John's and the Romare Beardom's? They are gone. They have been replaced with cheesy cartoon style "art" that was inspired by Japanese animated style art.

Allen Ginsberg has been relegated to the "Quaint, but Interesting" section of your local bookstore. No one wants to do the cut-up book of William S. Burroughs. Walter Mosley, Alexander McCauley Smith, and Sue Grafton and Alan Bradley have raised the bar so high in their genre that only the fearless of writers dare take up the literary gauntlet. This leaves the field of writing open for hack writers and washed- up ex boozers like Baltimore's "Blaster" Al Akerman or the late lame Anselm Hollo, or the man who calls himself "Karen Elliot".

This lack of vision is not only limited to "the Arts". It should be patently obvious that the official opposition political parties such as the Democratic Party in the United States of America not only do not have a vision of a world beyond capitalism, *and,* **DO NOT WISH** to even envision much less work for a world without capitalism. This goes even further for the Ayn Rand/ Libertarian/Populist/Fascists. Not only do these groups fail to have a vision of a world without capitalism, but they dream of a world with no restrictions at all on the capitalist money-grubbers. These people yearn for the bygone days of capitalism where the blood sucker Robber

Barons ruled the roost. Not only do these bloated toads yearn for this sad period of time, but they want to improve the fangs of the Dracula like Robber Barons so that they can suck more blood from their victims!

Now I can hear a choir of voices yelling "But what about the left"? Yeah, what about the left. Let's start with the anarchists. I remember talking to the multi-talented tENTATIVELY a cONVIENIENCE about his idea on how he would persuade someone who espoused a right-wing world outlook to unite with the left. He said he would tell this right-winger that anarchists *also* believed in a world with no government. From there he would then try and show how the best way to get rid of the state was to unite with anarchists and other forces of the left to do so. In other words, my friend "tent" saw political outlooks as a circle where anarchism and libertarianism met at one point and liberalism and social democrats met at another point, as opposed to a spectrum that went from left to right. I have extrapolated on this concept to say that this concept does not include the revolutionary communist outlook. In other words what you have in what I call the politics of despair or the politics of illusion. Should the person who looks for serious change within the electoral system, any turn towards the accepted routes of change will just be a vicious cycle, because nowhere in the circle of frauds will this searcher find an answer to their plight,

But wait say the voices of the left. *We* do have an alternative. Okay is that so? Let's start with the anarchists. How can a group of autonomous groupings overthrow or change the organized might of the state, when these autonomous groupings do not even dare to voice criticism of one another? This leads to this sad fact. The Dorothy Day Catholic Worker is anti-abortion and supports the legalization of narcotics by the very same organized government they wish to somehow abolish. [6] These anarchist groupings also say that the way to change things is through small incremental changes. However, in an age where the Bourgeoise is pushing *massive* backward quantum changes, how in the world can these baby step changes work? Then there is there are these other questions. What is to prevent a big autocoups grouping from gobbling up smaller communities in the anarchist world? And think about this. What is there to prevent an anarchist honcho from turning the autonomous group into his fiefdom using the theory that whatever change is premature? I remember hearing a self-defined "Zen -Anarchist" at a meeting of the Baltimore Ethical Society say that both affirmative action and a federal minimum wage are harmful to workers. This WHITE MAN said that having a minimum wage hurts Black people the hardest because the potential employer can't hire more Black and other minority people. (Then according to this logic, this Zen Anarchist would uphold slavery. That way the potential employer could not be restricted by the constrictions of paying the slaves any wages at all. And as a matter of fact, this WHITE MAN and a buddy of HIS were both opposed to affirmative action, because he said: "You can't pass a law to make people *like you* -sic)

Then you have the Anarcho-Syndicalists. With all their who- hah about abolishing the wage system, they have no *real* alternative to capitalism. All they want to do is have one big union. That's fine in theory. No that isn't fine in theory. Why is that? That is because even in this big union, all the locals are autonomous. I remember talking to the late radio activist Howard Ehrlich (sp?) that the Great Atlantic Radio Conspiracy

---

[6] I have heard a K. Boylan espouse this program on the Washington radio station W.P.F.W.

I.W.W collective was told by the I.W.W. central command that his local was too big and this group had to split into two autocoups groupings! And then there is the sad fact that these Anarcho-Syndicalist see everybody as a "worker". That means that people who are forced into selling their bodies for sex are not prostitutes, but "Sex Workers". That is because these misguided people or want to be pimps want to coddle the victims of capitalism into thinking what they do puts the prostitute into the working class! If prostitutes are "SEX WORKERS" are pimps SEX ENTRAPANOURS?

Then you have all of those leftist "socialist" and "Labor" groups. You know the Workers World Party, The Socialist Workers Party, The Progressive Labor Party, The Party for Socialism and Unity, The Socialist Unity Party, and so on and so on. Now I am not red-baiting, however, each of these groups claims to be at least a Marxist Party. (The Socialist Labor Party says they are a Marxist "humanist" Party) and except for the Progressive Labor that calls itself a "Revolutionary Communist Party" none of them openly espouse the communist essence of their communism. At this point I must give props to the Communist Party U.S.A at least they have the nerve despite their economist politics and their slavish devotion to electoral politics this party calls itself a communist party. (As opposed to the long-gone Communist Workers Party and the defunct Communist Labor Party and the defunct Communist Party Marxist Leninist or the other deceased new communist groups who lost faith in what they claimed to espouse when capitalism was restored in China.) However, what these groups have in common is they are bound to the electoral road for change (Except for the Progressive Labor Party) And once again except the

Progressive Labor that has some sort of idea that socialism and the dictatorship of the proletariat are now obsolete (Yeah right!) all of these groups have no real idea of what a world without capitalism is all about, much less how this workers' paradise can be brought into being through the ballot box, much less evolve into a withering away of the state! And so, as they have the working class running around chasing their tails the Bourgeoise sing to the tune of the Dion song The Wanderer

"We're the kind of class that likes to keep the people down

In each and every land we always can be found

We rob folks and cheat folks and push their noses to the ground

We shoot kill those oppose us so that they don't make as sound

'Cause we're the bourgeoise

We're the bourgeoise

We exploit around -around -around"

So, what does this have to do with the arts? It's quite simple. Without a left that has an artistic Vision (with a capital V) and a view of the world beyond a tired view of socialism that does not include the dictatorship of the Proletariat, you will have a kind of dull if not vapid kind of culture. This is because these lefties can't think beyond movies like Salt of the Earth or Norma Rae or the militant trade unionism of Woody Guthrie or The Weavers songs like This Land is Your Land. These groups have no poetic Vision no artistic Vision and no Vision that is more political than union songs or folk style songs. And to be perfectly frank if the potential revolutionary wants to be a revolutionary leader that leader must be a poet like Mao or have a poetic side-then that potential leader can't or will not be in a position to give the leadership of a revolutionary movement.

How does this impact on the culture of the times? Well back in the sixties, the culture was more vibrant. In spite of more than a bit of white chauvinism, the rock/acid rock/the blues-rock and other rock forms were more vibrant and more interesting. Jazz artists were more pushing the envelope of the music. European and American "Classical: composers like John Cage, Edgar Varese, Leonard Bernstein were exploring new ways to compose. While this was going on you had The Great Proletarian Cultural Revolution in China inspiring revolutionaries around the world. The rippling effect created in the creation of Maoist groups like The Black Panther Party, The Young Lords the Revolutionary Union (Which became the Revolutionary Communist Party), and some members of the Students for a Democratic Society.

With the overthrow of communism, China and the blatant betrayal of socialism in Cuba-the the culture of struggle became less vital. In opposition to Max Roach and Archie Shepp recording compositions Suite Mao and The Long March, you had Prairie Fire recording songs like "Come on Vergie We're Going Out on Strike" and the lackluster sing-along songs of Holly Near.

Was it any wonder that the eighties produced Punk Rock, Rap, and Hip Hop? And was it any wonder that those who produced the music corrupted rap and hip hop into the drivel it has become? MTV became the Sominex of music. However, despite the creation of this gangsta and ego rap you have the constantly evolving group Public Enemy and the new fresh Outernational taking care of business and putting out some righteous sounds.

So, what does this have to do with the nature of Jig Saw writing or anything I have done? It's simple. In one of the Orpheus movies by Jean Cocteau, the poet asks his friend what the poet should do. The friend "amaze people" That's what the modern poet/artist writer musician /composer should do. Let me go further. It would far better for the modern folk singer to perform the John Cage composition 4:33 than Union Maid! Why is that? Because 4:33 the listener to listen and to appreciate the presence of unorganized sound, and to reevaluate what sound is, as opposed to the call to workers to "get you a man who's a union man and join the ladies auxiliary" (the original lyrics) or "look for the union label" "the union makes us strong" (This lyric is especially vapid given the sorry state and history of trade unionism. Seriously do you really expect to tell workers that "the union makes you strong"? No, the union does not make you strong! The union just put you in a tenuous bargaining from a position of weakness for a few crumbs from their employers that can be snatched away at their first opportunity. Singing this song is especially odious when people who call themselves leftists when it was Lenin who seriously downplayed the role of "The Trade Union Secretary and urged people to be "TRIBUNES OF THE PEOPLE![7])

So, what should the modern creative soul do? Well first of all look around. Look at the films of Jean Luc Goddard or David Lynch and take their examples to make more political films. Take a tip from William S, Burroughs and remove the misogamy and do something better with his cut-up style. Learn from Kenneth Carroll and Amari Baraka or Allice Walker. (Just do not become a 911 truther if, in fact, she is one. Listen to the Electric Miles Davis. Listen to the old fashioned Karlheinz Stockhausen. Think outside thinking outside the box! Stop writing for the 99% and just write. Put the cultural elite and culture vultures on notice that these folks do *not* control culture. Stop letting the dregs of cover bands bar bands cowboy hat-wearing red neckbands, bubble gum pop bands disco bands with their light laser shows, and poisonous designer drugs keep their crap on center stage. We have to say AWAY WITH ALL RAVES!

---

[7] Read it in What is to be Done?

AWAY WITH ALL PORN AND SUB PORN FRONTING OFF AS "EROTICA"!

AWAY WITH ALL, THAT IS DULL!

AWAY WITH SOMINEX CULTURE! AWAY WITH POLITE CULTURE!

AWAY WITH COMPUTER-GENERATED DULL CULTURE.

ANYTHING THAT MAKES THE POWERS BE FEEL RELAXED

Roque Dalton said those who hold power see the poet as a friend, a clown, or as the enemy!

Don't be their friend!

Don't be their clown That means do not be their court jester!

Be their enemy!

NEVER COMPROMISE WITH THE LACKLUSTER TRENDS IN YOUR BEING!

CREATE TO AMAZE!

CREAT TO CONFUSE THE TEPID!

CREATE TO INSPIRE!

CREAT!

CREAT!

CREAT!

And never-ever give long-winded to your poems at an open mike!

ALWAYS GIVE YOUR CREATIONS ROOM TO SPEAK FOR THEMSELVES!

CREATE!

CREATE!

CREATE!

STAND YOUR ARTISTIC GROUND!

CREATE!

 CREATE!

LET AMBIENT MUSIC EMPOWER ORGANIZED SOUND!

CREATE EVEN IF NO ONE ELSE HAS CAUGHT UP TO YOU!

REMEMBER TO HOLLAR BECAUSE THE TOWN IS NOT TO SMALL!

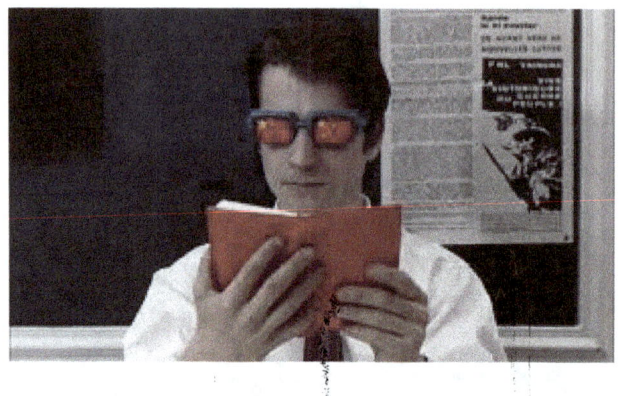

FIN!

Afterthought

When Miles Davis recorded Some Day, My Prince Will Come he did not have the traditional liner notes. He preferred to let the music speak for itself! Writers should give the same respect for their words as Miles Davis did for his music. Picasso did the same with his art. Martha Graham did the same with her dance performances. If it worked for these giants, you could try to do this for you! (most of the time)

Preface

The composer Edgar Varese told me once not to worry about what other people thought about his music. He told me these people listened to music "Their memories only" And so I tell you, Bob Avakian do not worry about what opportunists think about your politics. They analyze the situation of the current world situation with their memories only

CHAPTER FIVE

On Myths, Religion, and Other ways to Reign in "The Flock"

An Open Letter to Bob Avakian

Dear Chairman, Avakian

In your book The New Communism, you point out that if left to their own devices people can become the victims of deception and self-deception. This thought speaks volumes. I would like at this time to expand on this observation.

Deception has always been one way those on top have been able to deceive people into doing their bidding. One of the ways the oppressor uses to keep people stupid is mythology. From the first tribes to the fascist leaders of today myths, are one way those who had ruled from above-kept order in the order of things. Myths have also been used as a way to justify one nation oppressing another. The Nazis always upheld a bunch of gobeldy goop about the historical Nordic /Aryan race. This dangerous ideology has spawned neo -Neanderthals marching and yelling "Blood and Soil" in Charleston. This is the same ideology that the Fascists and Nazis of the past have used to justify war and genocide.

Let me give you an example. Take some dumb German yokel from some backwater German hick town who has returned from the First World War. He has no job. The economy has tanked. Then along come so sociopath who tells him that you are not a victim of s system, but a superman that has been kicked to the curb by a cabal of evil people. Now, this sociopath tells this dumb schmuck that he comes from a master race, and in order to run the con this manipulator of turkeys comes up with some stupid story. Maybe it's a Nordic or Gothic or Italian or some cultural nationalist/Nation of Islam science fiction/lethal fairy tale, but the results are the same. The leader tells the rube this story, and the poor dim-whit takes the wool and pulls it over his or her own head, puts a dog collar on, and hands the con man the leash. Hitler had the master race. The southern cracker has the south shall rise again. Minister Louis Farrakhan has his theory. Doctor Francis Welsing has her children of the son theory, which is the mirror image of the Jack London children of the cold theory. Whatever theory they have, these theories are like left shoes, there is nothing right about them! This however is not the only theory that these reactionaries are running. They need to create the other. They need to tell the stupid yokel just why he or she is the fit caretaker of the world. That requires more pseudo-science. Then you get the theory of the mud people, the theory of the savage northern people who can't survive in the cold, the theory of noble people who can survive the cold, the theory of the noble people of the sun, the theory of the southern savage, and when you really want to bamboozle the people the theory of some evil scientist who made daemons, who looked white or were mud people. These toxic fairy tales have another trait. They are almost all misogynistic, homophobic or anti-Semitic in one form or another, and either explicitly or implicitly justify the other people should be eliminated one way or another and oppose "race-mixing"

And there you have it. Then the leader has the flock in the palm of his hand. With the flock in tow, this leader then needs other ways to keep the faithful. This is done by forcing the faithful to be faithful. The first was financial. The leader always to tell the flock that if the faithful do *not* cough up some Scheckel's all hell will break loose, and the fate of the minister, the flock, the world, and perhaps the universe will be lost if not for a bit of time, then forever. Then after that is done, the leader must shove rituals up the asses of the faithful. Ramadan, praying while facing mecca, genital mutilation, giving something up for a month, fasting and diet are ways the leader keeps being the leaser. Another way of doing this is through diet. The leader tells the flock don't eat pork, don't drink alcohol, etc. One of the most vicious is the imposition of veganism on the flock. Veganism deprives the human body of natural animal protein needed to survive and to think more rationally. A vegan diet causes less blood to flow to the brain, thus making the brain less likely to think rationally. This is why the members of the Unification Church or the Hari Krishna's' act so zombie-like. This is why cultural nationalists keep the faithful in tow.

A case for example is a woman who calls herself "Doctor" Sunnyatta Amen. Even though there is no proof that she is a doctor, she was allowed to run her mouth off on both the Fox network and the Pacifica Radio network until under great pressure the programmer of W.P.F.W. told her she could not call herself Doctor and her host on the Fox network was booted off the airwaves. And on the station, W.P.F.W. two on-air programmers who should have known better came to this woman's defense. I know, they personally verbally attacked me. The talk show host J. Winter Night-wolf tried to say I was "racist" for this act. His social-democratic side kick Joanie Eisenberg fell in lockstep without even looking into this question. That is the power of cult leaders on their flock.

These cults that I have mentioned are toxic, and their toxicity flows into the minds of the faithful. Be they Alt-right, fascist white nationalist, the Nation of Islam, the Moorish American Church, The New Hebrew Israelites, the Hari Krishna's' or the "God loves Nixon" Unification Church diet and myth are used to control the people who need to be controlled. And it works. Be this some Chinese fundamentalist sect or the followers of the Dali Lama or the Nazis or The Moonies it's a one size fits all scheme. The enemy is always another race, or religion, or sexual orientation or worst of all a one worlder or communist. Fetuses become children, science, and evolutionary science, in particular, are debunked and rational thinking is debunked. For example, all these groups believe in an end-times theory. I would bet that these groups believe all the conspiracy theories the right-wing populist movement holds near and dear to their wizzled hearts. For example, the Minister Louis Farrakhan quoted chapter and verse the theory that 9/11 was an inside job from the cockeyed talk show host Alex Jones.

What do revolutionaries do when faced with people who are attracted to the revolutionary cause but still cling to these theories. Well, the answer is clear. We must be scientific and tell them these truths in a much more detailed way. We have to say the earth is not a basement workshop for evil scientists. We have to say there are no mud people. We have to say the climate does not determine the humanity of an individual. People not space aliens built the pyramids and other things like that. The earth is round, neither the God they worship, or Satan exists, and the economic system called capitalism is the source of their problems, not some secret society. That is because if that were the case, all revolutionaries would have to do is take over these societies and everything would be peachy keen. Then to those who say there is nothing we can do because these secret societies have everything under control we have to try and win them over or just walk away and hope that after the seizure of state power we can show them through reality that they were wrong.

Along with these toxic cults and reactionary heritage theories you have the silly, there are silly theories like the ones that people have that celebrate Beltane. While these people are not reactionaries, they are not doing much good just waltzing around a May Pole. However, these folks do love nature! These people can be united around the stop around stopping the attacks on the environment. There are parts of the Draft Constitution about not surprising religion, that is not actively organizing to overthrow the new government.

Having said that, I would like to return to how the cults of toxicity control their flock. The main way they do this is fear. I have pointed out how fear of the "others" is used. However, there is another fear that is used. That is a fear of punishment in "The After Life" That is where the invisible enemy comes in. Face it if the God these people is to be considered an invisible friend, why isn't Satan considered an invisible foe? And. If telling people to either do nothing in this world but await some big wingding that will call them up to the Pearly Gates Estates (The Oldest Gated Community in the Universe). However, this is not enough to keep the flock in line. Fear is also a must. Didn't John Calvin call people "Sinners in the hand of an angry God"? The Quran starts off telling the faithful how bad things will be should they piss off Allah. Then there is Satan! I do believe this negative fairy tell character has an even worse reputation than communism has among the ranks of "the faithful". Why is that? Well, communism is of "this world", and hell is forever! Now, who under the spell or influence of a man of God would want to get lakefront property on the lake of Sulphur and brimstone, when you could get a good condo where you would never grow old?

This brings us to dogma. We have seen this in the church. You know that give me that old-time religion hogwash. It was good enough for so and so- it is good enough for me! However, you have pointed out in your landmark thesis the New Communism that this kind of thinking is not one that should have a home in the real world. And, that is why the revisionists revile you!

Face it my comrade why would anyone with visions of their own grandeur want to admit that some upstart to prove them wrong? That is why they cling to the theories that have made them feel secure! For example, the idea that whatever happened in the past communist revolutions is the best and the only solution for the future of humanity.

I remember watching the reruns of the Ernie Kovacs show where whenever there was a commercial someone would yell "Hold it right there, don't go no further!". That is also the way the revisionists look at communist theory. I remember when there was a Party branch in my hometown, the grouping that split from the Party kept asking me why I read all the things I read/ They openly wondered how I could keep things straight. Many a time I would be asked "How are you going to understand the correct line if you read that other stuff too?" or worse. When it became patently obvious after reading Revolutionary Work in a Non-Revolutionary Situation that reading What is to be done? should be of the utmost priority on people's reading lists. What did this clique tell me? "Workers don't have time to read stuff like that" This restrictive thinking has and is and will always be how revisionist operate.

That is why revisionists like to water down or "creatively apply "the science to fit their agendas. So that instead of calling capitalists - capitalists they call capitalists "bosses" Instead of calling their parties Communist -they call them "Workers" or "Socialist" or "Labor" parties. That's because the toxic fear of an anti-communist backlash coupled with the poisonous legacy of revisionism has empowered these misleaders to cowardly foist their views on those they wish to corral and bludgeon into their ranks.

Along with this lack of vision of the revisionist comes their solutions that patently fly in the face of the true revolutionary science. That is why the slogans' money for (fill in the blank) not war is so popular in the ranks of the respectable left. As one representative of the Workers World Party asked me "How do expect to recruit your average welfare mother into the struggle if you won't recruit her into the struggle for jobs?" The reformist activist Phyllis Bennis told me that the half a loaf is better than none was okay. She even said that it would be okay to continue wars of aggression with less funding should "the people" get bigger crumbs from the bourgeoise.

This is because the respectable left has no vision of a world without capitalism. They trot out phrases like you can't expect things to change overnight. True you can't expect to change anything-not even your socks. However, you can and should work to change things. And sometimes as we see things change overnight due to the very workings of the direction of history as in the events surrounding the police murder of George Floyd.

Coupled with this fear of losing control of their flock is the sterile view of socialism and the non-visionary view that somewhere over the rainbow millions or billions of years in the future we will arrive at a color-blind leaderless communist world.

I shudder to think of a world like that. I agree with Carl Dix that we work for a colorful world. I agree with Reverend David Carl Olson that we do not need a leaderless world, but a leader full world. Let the revisionists paint socialism in dull grey colors, while we describe socialism as a great time of upsurge and struggle. Let the respectable left try and sell pablum as steak and water as grape juice, while communists portray communism as what it is.

Communists have to portray the future we aspire to as a joyous, erotic, and even yes psychedelic world where humanity is unfettered by anything, and we can even evolve into a post-communist world! We have to not only think outside the box but think outside the outside of the box! When breaking with the past we who sing of the future electric must make a clean sharp break from anything and any tactic and idea that will inhibit the advancement of humanity and the planet. I know I must have raised an eyebrow when I said that the future should be described as psychedelic. I do not mean a world where people are tripped out and gazing at watermarks on paper saying, "groovy man". I mean a world where beauty and love are in command. This is the world where all forms of healing including what were formerly abused "recreational" drugs are used to heal medical problems that formerly used regular cures were used as in the case of Aldous Huxley and Carry Grant or marijuana is now used to treat depression and anxiety today. We have to continue to let a hundred flowers bloom and go even further to make millions of flowers bloom! To be frank, the future belongs to the visionaries only if they act like visionaries and work as it does. The future is still uncertain. However, this future we aspire to must be struggled for. Yes, it still is a long shot. However, as you and Carl Dix say it's the only shot, WE have!

En Lucha/In Struggle

Alan Barysh

CHAPTER SIX

The Jean Luc-Goddard Cinematic Ending

I wish I knew how

It would feel to be free

I wish I could break

All the chains holding me

I wish I could say

All the things that I should say

Say 'em loud, say 'em clear

For the whole round world to hear

I wish I could share

All the love that's in my heart

Remove all the bars

That keep us apart

I wish you could know

What it means to be me

Then you'd see and agree

That everyone should be free

I wish I could give

All I'm longin' to give

I wish I could live

Like I'm longin' to live

I wish I could do

All the things that I can do

And though I'm way overdue

I'd be starting anew

Well, I wish I could be

Like a bird in the sky

How sweet it would be

If I found I could fly

Oh I'd soar to the sun

And look down at the sea

Then I'd sing 'cause I know, yea

Then I'd sing 'cause I know, yea

Then I'd sing 'cause I know

I'd know how it feels

Oh I know how it feels to be free

Yea yea! Oh, I know how it feels

Yes, I know, oh, I know

How it feels

How it feels

To be free, Lord, Lord, Lord

Fight The Power

Public Enemy

Yet our best trained, best educated, best equipped, best-prepared troops refuse to fight
As a matter of fact, it's safe to say that they would rather switch than fight
1989 the number another summer (get down)
Sound of the funky drummer
Music hitting your heart 'cause I know you got soul
(Brothers and sisters, hey)
Listen if you're missing y'all
Swinging while I'm singing
Giving whatcha getting
Knowing what I know
While the Black bands sweatin'
And the rhythm rhymes rollin'
Got to give us what we want (uh)
Gotta give us what we need (hey)
Our freedom of speech is freedom or death
We got to fight the powers that be
Lemme hear you say
Fight the power (lemme hear you say)
Fight the power
Fight the power
Fight the power
Fight the power
Fight the power
Fight the power
We've got to fight the powers that be
As the rhythm designed to bounce
What counts is that the rhymes
Designed to fill your mind
Now that you've realized the pride's arrived
We got to pump the stuff to make us tough
From the heart

It's a start, a work of art
To revolutionize make a change nothing's strange
People, people we are the same No, we're not the same
'Cause we don't know the game
What we need is awareness, we can't get careless
You say what is this?
My beloved let's get down to business
Mental self-defensive fitness
(Yo) bum rush the show
You gotta go for what you know
To make everybody see, in order to fight the powers that be
Lemme hear you say
Fight the power (lemme hear you say)
Fight the power
Fight the power
Fight the power
Fight the power
Fight the power
Fight the power
We've got to fight the powers that be
Fight the power (lemme hear you say)
Fight the power
Fight the power
Fight the power
Fight the power
Fight the power
We've got to fight the powers that be
Elvis was a hero to most but he
Elvis was a hero to most
Elvis was a hero to most
But he never meant shit to me you see
Straight up racist that sucker was
Simple and plain
Mother fuck him and John Wayne
'Cause I'm Black and I'm proud
I'm ready and hyped plus I'm amped
Most of my heroes don't appear on no stamps
Sample a look back you look and find
Nothing but rednecks for four hundred years if you check

Don't worry be happy
Was a number one jam
Damn if I say it you can slap me right here
(Get it) let's get this party started right
Right on, c'mon
What we got to say (yeah)
Power to the people no delay
Make everybody see
In order to fight the powers that be
Fight the power
Fight the power
Fight the power
Fight the power
We've got to fight the powers that be
What have we got to say? (yeah)
Fight the power (yeah, yeah, yeah)
What have we got to say? (yeah)
Fight the power (come on)
What have we got to say? (yeah)
Fight the power (yeah, yeah, yeah)
What have we got to say? (yeah)
Fight the power (come on)
Yo check this out man
OK talk to me about the future of Public Enemy
The future of Public Enemy gotta
Source: Lyric Find
Songwriters: Carlton Ridnour / Eric Sadler / Hank Shocklee /

The Internationale   [variant words in square brackets]

Arise ye workers [starvelings] from your slumbers
Arise ye prisoners of want
For reason in revolt now thunders
And at last, ends the age of cant.
Away with all your superstitions
Servile masses arise, arise
We'll change henceforth [forthwith] the old tradition [conditions]
And spurn the dust to win the prize.

So, comrades, come rally
And the last fight let us face
The Internationale unites the human race.
So, comrades, come rally
And the last fight let us face
The Internationale unites the human race.

No more deluded by reaction
On tyrants only we'll make war
The soldiers too will take strike action
They'll break ranks and fight no more
And if those cannibals keep trying
To sacrifice us to their pride
They soon shall hear the bullets flying
We'll shoot the generals on our own side.

No saviour from on high delivers
No faith have we in prince or peer
Our own right hand the chains must shiver
Chains of hatred, greed and fear
E'er the thieves will out with their booty [give up their booty]
And give to all a happier lot.
Each [those] at the forge must do their duty
And we'll strike while the iron is hot.

The Big Book About Sounds

Plagiarized from a Talk by Bob Avakian at a Black Panther Rally

Okay I want to talk to you white people today

As you know those who speak for the Black Lives Matter movement have said they don't hate you because you are white. Then you think well that means I can go back to business as usual. My life is all right. Well, if you think like that our sisters and brothers in the Black Lives Matter movement won't hate you because you're white! They will hate you because you ain't taking care of business the business of standing up against a rotten ass system that is racist to the core!

On Time, "Silence" and Space[8]

Or

The Growing Importance of 4:33

Part One

Speed Kills!

In the poems of mine, do I Have the Time? And Nodal Points I explore the idea of time as a flexible idea. In these brief mental wanderings, I explore the concept of time expanding and contracting depending on the circumstances. For example, there is what I will call the seconds before lover's ecstasy are: long, anxious, hopeful, and full of ecstasy. Just as when one is listing to a talk by Noam Chomsky time slows down so slowly that giant three towed sloths can walk their lives away, before Mr. Chomsky has read a paragraph.

Time has always been described in a number of ways. In my book where I interview the characters that I write about this is what Father Time has to say

Father Time Says His piece
"Let's take our hearts out for a walk through the autumn woods and listen to the magic of the trees"

Unknown author's Facebook Page Post

Alan Barysh: Good evening Mr. Time. I understand that you also have a prepared statement. It would give me great pleasure to hear this statement. Mr. Time, the stage is yours.

---

[8] This is yet another reprint from a book by this author called The New Space and Time. It is reprinted here as is and before your author started calling himself in the second person.

Father Time: My name is father time.

I'm on the B list

Be here before you were born

Be here when you leave this life.

I was here before a creator mad life

Or

before life created the creator.

(I leave that for another talk)

I come in all forms

I am hard time

I am difficult time

I am lean times

I am fat and good times.

Often enough I am what you make me.

It took me centuries to make the glaciers or the mountains.

It took you seconds to strip mine and pollute.

I was used in creating the atom

You squandered me making nuclear waste.

If you use me wisely the sun in the sky would energize your world

Oil would still be where it should be

My redwood trees growing

History would be different.

But you humans squander me

You watch too much Star Wars stuff

You could be traveling through me and through space.

Instead, you openly talk about killing me

You never talk about using me wisely

You don't know just how much you need me.

I ferment your wine

I grow your yogurt

Eventually, I heal all wounds

At times I am right for you

(In spite of what you think.)

Without me nothing grows or dies.

I was there when light the first dawn of light shined over the waters.

I listened to new sounds in the trees.

I keep memories for you.

I turn diamonds into coal

I make grapes raisins and now into history.

Now, humans, I say

Use me wisely

Use me with a future in mind.

I am always in abundance.

That does not mean I can be squandered.

Move when the time is urgent

Rest when you have the need.

Do not however throw me out with the morning paper.

You might be somewhere where you need me and can't find me.

When the bottle breaks the insides just keep spilling along!

The Big Book About Sounds

Alan Barysh: Thank you Mr. Time. I'll get back to you later.

Father Time: Please do, I have all the stuff you need.

(Sound of a tape recorder being turned off)

The Beginning of the Eisenstein Like Interlude in the spirit of the ending of "Ten days that Shook The World"

What time does the clock show?

:00

Do I have the time?[9]

---

[9] This is a newly revised version of this poem/rant. An earlier version may be found on either the compact disk or book by Alan Barysh-Art Between Deliveries on Amazon.com

Dedicated to Markus Sanders and Jenefer Keith-Ciatti

For the time being, I can't afford to have writer's block

I am being chased at all times by the obsession to get everything down and get it out!

There is no time for the luxury of self-editing

The clock is ticking away

It all must get out on paper.

Someone else will figure out what is good

I should be so lucky

The only question I have is do I have the time?

Do I have the time?

Is anyone listening?

I feel trapped

I feel that I am trapped.

I feel as though I am surrounded by jackals and bullies, the language police members of the "Woke Patrol" Christian Fascists, Gandhian Fascists, Libertarian Fascists, and anarchist "anti-authoritarian" who are out to see that I am "politically under control" and want to run my life like a bad circus.

Do I have the time?

Each and Every day I read where some spoiled brat with a synthesizer and a cute little lost puppy look that always helped a looser like Jim Morrison become the new lord -high anti-Peter Pan for a generation of flower-girl/children who mistook him for Jesus is now being hailed as

The next greatest thing

Greater than anyone

Except

Elvis

And that self-destructive

Skin peeling

Monkey loving

Land-lord of Neverland

Little Mike Jackson

Who should have listened to The man in the mirror"

And will always find a home in the arms of people with more money than musical or artistic taste.

Every day I see a clone of a clone of a clone being hailed as though his washed-up rhetoric was the Newest "Bestist "Thing

To be dished out in dog food bowls as if were mana from heaven.

And I still write

And I still go one

And the clock ticks

And the pink boys and girls and the little lost snowflakes snicker and laugh

All the while the "Wolk Folk " argue way too long about what pronoun they want others to call them behind their back

While they are oblivious to any real threats to their little Kingdoms or Queendomes

These "woke folk" are really new aga somnambulists stumbling over their own dull rhetoric

Saying that no one knows how bad they have it

Once they might have sung better songs

But now they yell "cancel" and insist that the song

"Nobody Know The Trouble I've Seen"

Become not a mantra for themselves

But the word of a tran-creature deity that should be believed.

(The word should has replaced must

The word police think the word must is too forceful.

This is not the only thing the word police do

They have ousted the word but

They claim it is too forceful

Complimenting children has been acuminated by the prose popes

This is a lie

This is not true

He is lying

She is lying all have been replaced with I think etc before the phrase he/she/ is lying

However woe be unto the un-woke who call prostitutes -prostitutes not "sex Workers"

Worker in the pig's eye

Ain't too many of us workers 'round today

We are wage -slaves pure and simple)

And time goes on

The Vegan Vigalanties picket dairy farms protesting the fact cows are artificially inseminated and can not enjoy an orgasm

Peter Singer got involved with animal husbandry

"Until they caught him at it" Tom Leher

And restaurants are picketed by pixies and their hipster comrades who all look like they could use a good meal)

The hands of time keep moving around

The numbers of the increments of time flip over and over like those schedule updates in the railroad station

All the while a disembodied voice announces the passage of a passage in time

A passage of time lost in the universe

A passage of time that more than likely never be able to brag about what was going on in their little moment flash

Let alone in universal history

I push out words in a jumble

They spill out like those numbered/lettered children's blocks that fall together making words and sentences

Doubt is sitting on my shoulder looking very much like a winged -monkey in a bell-hop-suit.

doubt is constantly holding cue cards in my face

Cue cards that say

"Is it worth it all at best they only want to laugh behind your back

At worst they will outright try to make everything you do say or think be used against you"

Just ask Heidi" says one sign

"Just ask Bambi," says another sign

Then jumping off my shoulder

Light as a hundred-pound weight

Starts jumping and twirling a dervish dance around my little Sears-Robuck model a-41 Kafkaesque Writers Loft (Some assembly required)

He is spinning like a little Richard spinning top

Like a dandy demon at a line dance

Like Martha Graham on Peyote

He leaps up in the air and clicks his heals together

While this is all going on

Father Time is whispering in my ears

Anything Father Time is saying is becoming more and more confusing to comprehend

All that can be heard are gurgling sounds and fish farts

Down the street, I hear the sounds of The Poet's Poet and His trusty comrade talking about poetry.

The Poet's poet is opening a box of Gallo Merlot and pouring it into red solo cups

While His trusty comrade in arms is smoking what only can be called a "skunk-weed reefer" It smells so downright awful

I gage on its smell even before it is blown out the open window a block or two upwind.

Then as if off cue, I hear music

It's the sound of a contrabass

The bass is being bowed

The music sounds Middle-Eastern

It sounds cyclical a weird ostinato a mysterioso pattern

Is it Ole or that song from the Spanish Civil War about Los Cuatro Generales

Or both

Then for a minute, my mind goes blank

The words trickle out of my ears and dribble down my cheek like liquid ear wax

There's no music in my mind

It's gone

All I hear is

A song called "It's a thriller to be an Okey From Miscoge"

Then the fate monkey holds a sign in my face

The sign says

"Is it really worth this effort?"

"Yes I Hollar

Darn tootin'

Uh-huh skippy

You got dat right

Sure as Shootin'

Why ?

Fool can't you hear the music of life is being played on that ole bass fiddle upstairs?

There comes a Time

"There Comes a time" Tony Williams

"If you live-your time will come" Mose Allison

There will come a time in your life when everything will telecsope down into

Time smaller than you can fathom

This will be a long time for you

Pressure builds

Time slows down

Should you wish you can hear

The universe inhalew

A green candle in a wine bottle being lit

A spark about to spark

Then in just a shaving of a second

Your world explodes with a joyous gush

Bodies become on with each other

Then one with nature and the universe

Then the universe itself

Then one with all energy and life forces

The the energy and life force of the universe

Then all ewnergies and life forces become you

Your souls explode with eros energy

Energy bright enough to illuminate black holes

Then this tooi subsides

Rest and joy return unto you

Satisfied smiles decorate your faces

Then a sly little angle whispersin your ear

"Don't look now

But somewhere in this universe

There's a star with your names on it"

Write the time.

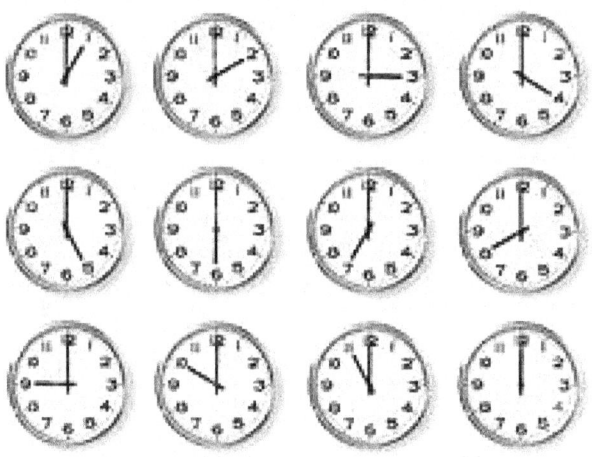

Name_____   Date_____

Identify Time to the Quarter Hour

What time does the clock show?

:00

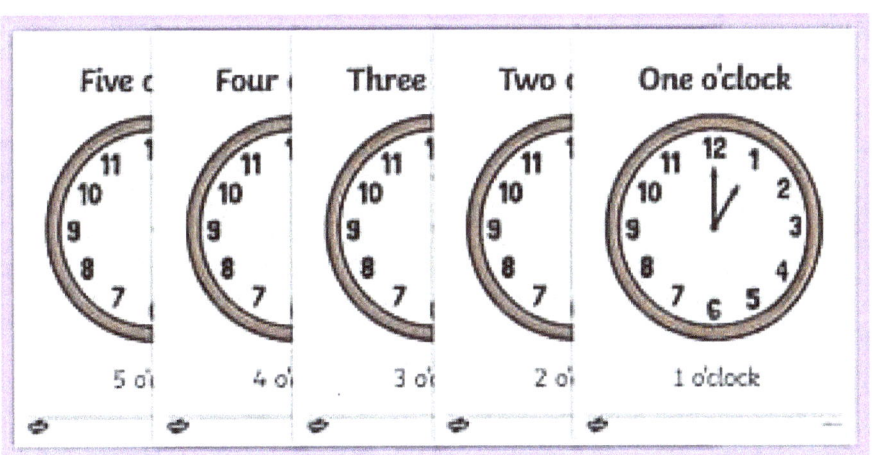

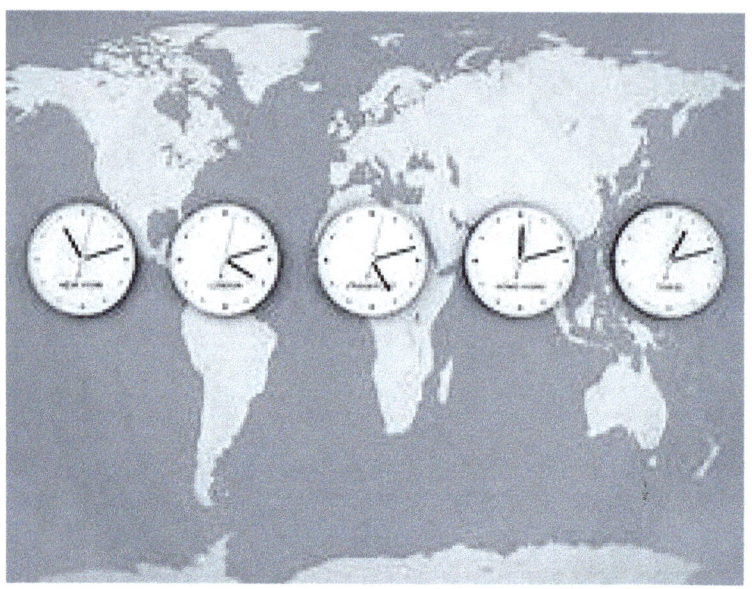

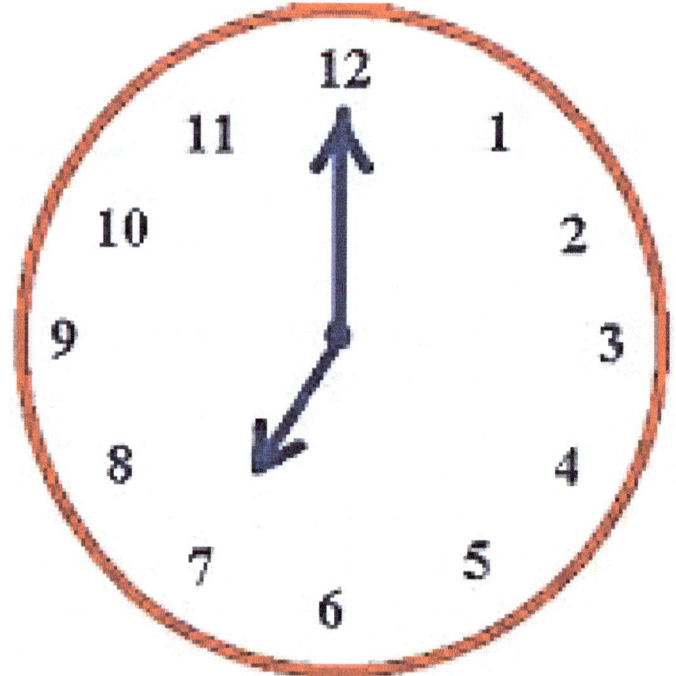

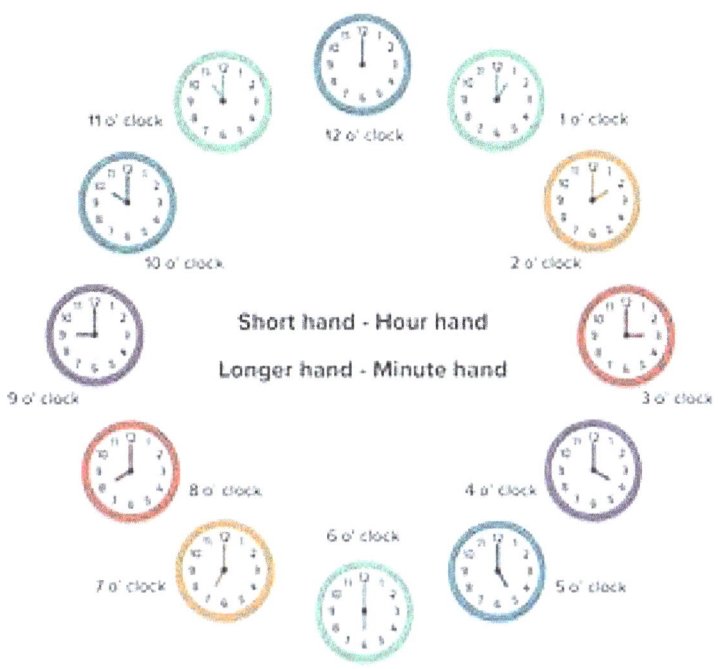

Short hand - Hour hand

Longer hand - Minute hand

Name _____ Date _____

Telling time Worksheet

Write the time.

1 a.	1 b.
2 a.	3 b.
5 a.	3 b.

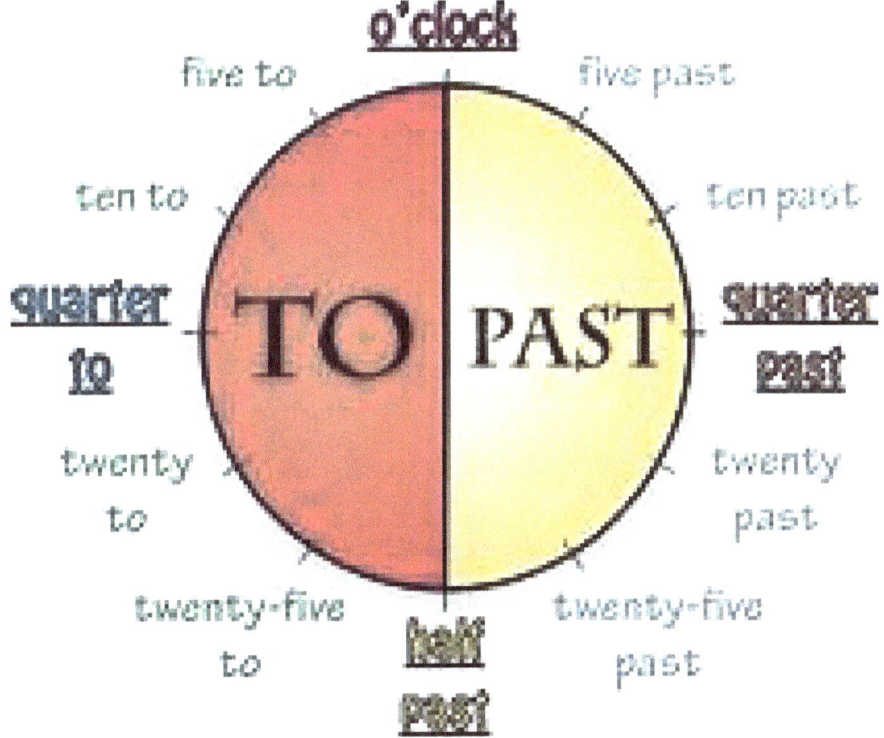

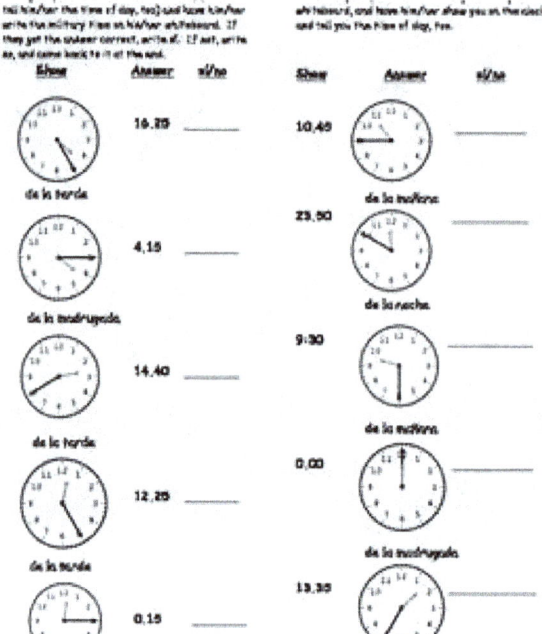

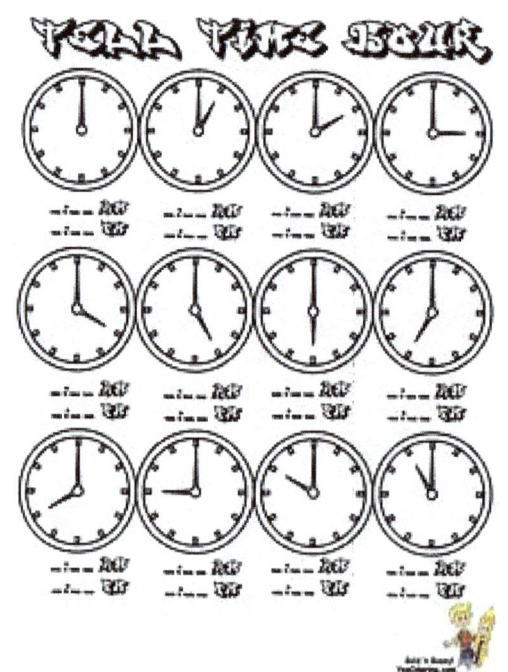

Which clock shows 10:30?

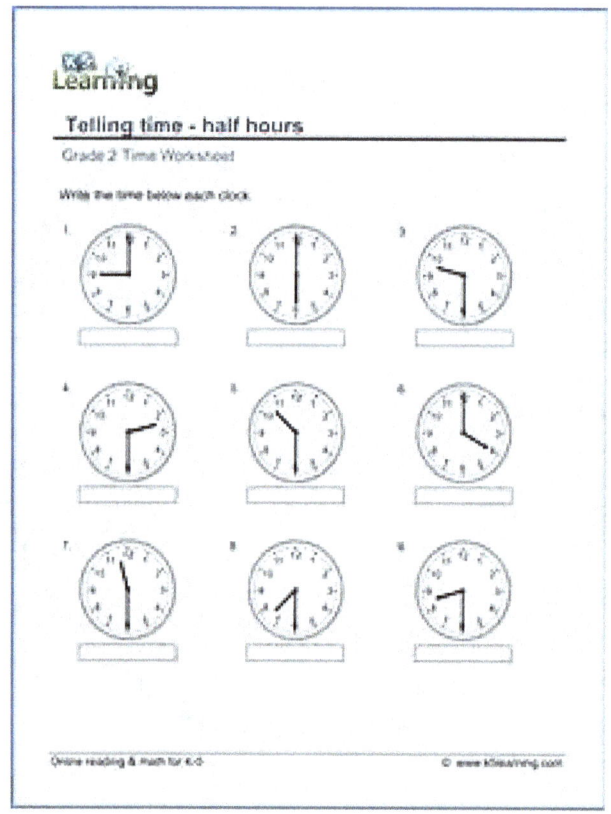

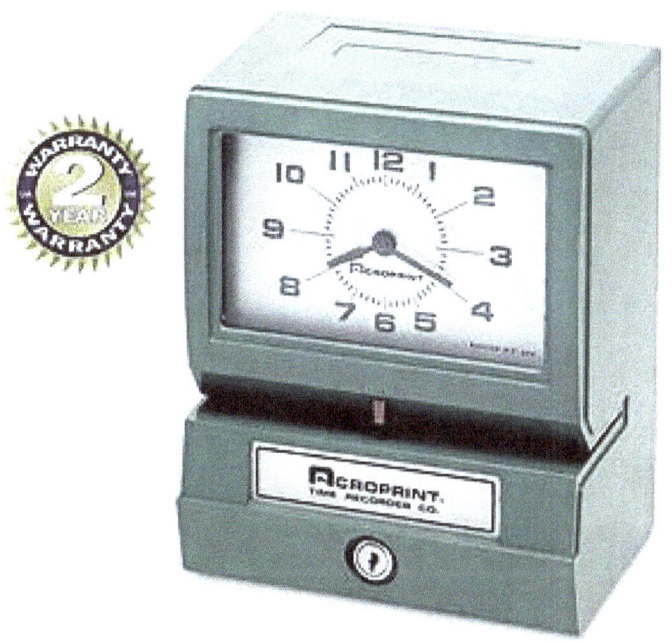

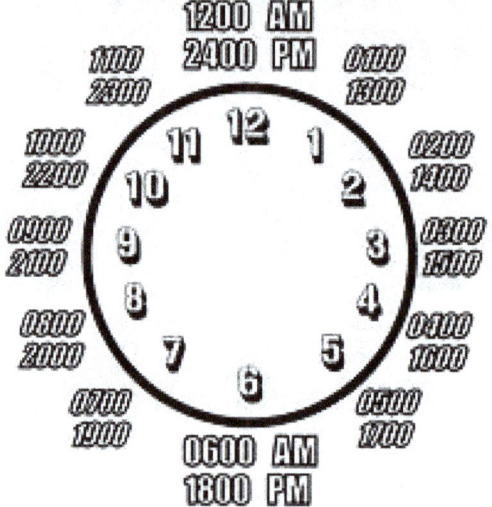

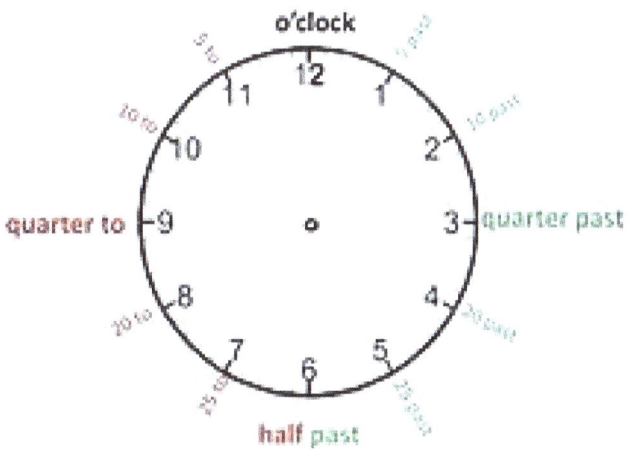

https://images.search.yahoo.com/images/view;_ylt=AwrExlR8q8peNp0Au.c2nIlQ;_ylu=X3oDMTIzY
mgxb3E1BHN1YwNzcgRzbGsDaW1nBG9pZAM5MDhlODAzOGQ1YjYyNjc4MWE2ZjM0ODVkMWZkZ
DRjYgRncG9zAzc1BGl0A2Jpbmc-
?back=https%3A%2F%2Fimages.search.yahoo.com%2Fyhs%2Fsearch%3Fp%3Dimages%2Bof%2Bcl
ocks%2Bwith%2Btime%2Bto%2Bthe%2Bhours%26fr%3Dyhs-Lkry-
SF01%26h%3D610%26hsimp%3Dyhs-
SF01%26hspart%3DLkry%26nost%3D1%26tt%3DOffice%2Bwall%2Bclock%2Bwith%2Bfull%2Bdays
%2Btime%2B...%2B%7C%2BStock%2Bvector%2B...%26w%3D800%26imgurl%3Dhttps%3A%2

- **Ending of the Eisenstein** Like Interlude in the spirit of the ending of **"Ten days that Shook The World"**

[Joe Lee Carter]{.underline} – Please Mr. Foreman Lyrics

Please Mr. Foreman... Slow down your assembly line
Please Mr. Foreman... Slow down your assembly line
You know I don't mind workin'
But I do mind dyin"

My wife is very sickly... You know she can't help me by taken on a job
My wife is very sickly... You know she can't help me by taken on a job
And we got five little children to feed
Lord why do you want to make my life so hard

Working 12 hours a day
Seven long days a week
I lay down and try to rest
But I'm too tired to sleep

Please Mr. Foreman... Why don't you slow down your assembly line
Lord you can look at me and see I don't mind workin'
Lord knows I do mind dyin"

Mr. Foreman Mr. Foreman why don't you slow down your assembly line
Yes my wife is very sickly
Whoa I can't feed my five little children when I come home
Yes every week I bring my paycheck home
Lord you know I catch a bus every day I do

This song reflects the dreary life of the proletariat, the assembly line worker. That life is one of speed. Everything is a rush. From the minute the assembly line worker gets up until quitting time, everything is on a rush-rush basis. The routine is the same. Rush to wake up. Then it's rushes to eat something (if at all possible). Then it's rushes to keep up with the assembly line. Do you doubt me? Why is the time going to work and coming home from work are called **RUSH HOURS**? Then it's rushes to eat lunch. Then back to work for more rushing around. When they let this worker go home, this worker rushes to a bar for a quick drink or home for dinner and some mindless entertainment. Then after that, sleep. Even when the assembly line worker has "time" off everything must be speed up to make use of the time. Speed and the need for speed are the burdens put on the shoulders of the working-class assembly line worker. Pleasant drinking sometimes is called getting a "quick one". Fast food has replaced what once was the art of the casual relaxed experience of dining out. Cooking has been eclipsed by heat and eat or food that can be nuked faster than ever. Shopping has become shop 'till you drop. The day after Thanksgiving-black Friday has perverted the phrase the early bird gets the worm to the sleepless bird gets the worm. The non-stop keep it up pressure has resulted in people bragging that "I'll sleep when I am dead." "Get it while you can" "Time and tide wait for no one!" Even lovemaking has been degraded to getting the meaningless and loveless "quickie". And should the natural energy a caffeinated beverage not suffice, the legal amphetamines in energy drinks or the drug called "*SPEED*" are there to fill the void of needed rest. No one remembers the phrase "You can't take it with you" "Get it while you can" is the mantra of the day. Even in other aspects of other workers lives things are not as bad. True you can get killed in after

The Big Book About Sounds

joining the armed forces in a war. However, my dad used to say that the tempo of military life in the Second World War was" Hurry up *and* wait.

This is just one example. People in the medical professions and service professions face the same need for speed. In times of crisis medical professionals must work tirelessly. Slow -down is not a phrase used in the service/restaurant business. I just chose autoworkers, because in spite of these workers doing their job at breakneck/sprit speeds most assembly lines are now outsourced to countries where things still dominated by the need for speed. Why think of this even childhood myths are slaves to the need to meet deadlines? Santa Clause has to work faster than Ups or Fed ex. That man has in theory to deliver goodies in a twenty-four-hour period. And he must work faster than Jack Bauer. Even Jack Bauer eats, sleeps, uses the John and hugs and kisses in his Twenty-four stint. Santa can't even relieve himself on a rooftop or call his wife. Ma God have mercy on the souls of the world should Santa pick up an assault rifle and go postal

The worst thing about working and living at a breakneck speed is you never have time to think or even breathe. Everything is a bit or byte. The symphony is gone. The casual walk has gone the way of the do -do bird. Daydreaming is not considered time well spent. Quality time has become quantity time. Lingering and lollygagging are frowned upon. Youth no longer are waiting for something to happen or hanging out. Chilling out is a joke. Why if Tolstoy were alive today, he'd have to cut down his War and Peace to either two haikus or a limerick. Yes, the life in the fast lane has increased the number of travelers so much that more people die in this area than people in all of the two World Wars. And speaking about speed, guess who invented or perfected the drug speed? The Nazis, so that their much-needed bomber pilots could make their bombing runs? (This is the subject of another bit of writing.)

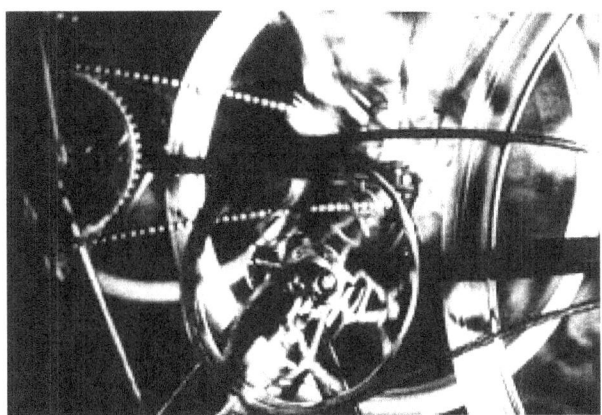

A super blood moon total lunar eclipse is seen in a composite
image taken in China on May 26, 2021.

CHAPTER SEVEN

Part Two

What's the Rush?

Or

John Cage to the Rescue (At a Leisurely Pace)
"Too many die, with the music in them"
Oliver Wendel Holmes

Now that we have exhausted the topic of speed, let's talk about rest and relaxation and the creative process. As I have said before. The bourgeoise needs workers who can work fast and go home just as quickly. In their world view, idle time is for the idle rich! Any form of creativity, intellectual curiosity and scientific ponderings are in an anthemia to capitalist class. However. These ideas are also not the things the *traditional* leftists and even anarchists' schools of thought. For the bourgeoisie un-changed thought leads questioning. For example, when Gutenberg invented moveable type, literacy for the masses was a reality. When Gallio invented the telescope the laws of the universe became clear to those who would dare to look. This translates to "Listen kid you ain't paid to think. You are paid to work!" or "I don't get paid to think!" Every capitalist and their lackie dreads the day when those who work under them will discover life outside of nine to five. For example, it is true that a section of the ruling class opted to support the new abstract art movement. However, even this form of art eluded the grip of the art police. Artist are artists. That means art encourages critical thinking and observing. Or to be quite frank do not look for a great deal of artists to be monolithic in their thought. That means Picasso can be a leftist. Norman Rockwell can be a leftist. But those paint brush hacks who painted portraits of Hitler were Nazis.

Now let's look at the traditional left. Let's take social realism. Social realism was started to also oppose the abstract art movement. This stereotyped picture of the mussel bound workers beating the exceeded quotas just makes these old lefties cry like babies. Now there is a need for stirring artwork. A bold cry to defend the future is what the world needs now. However, the traditional left likes to micro-manage the creative thought process of the people they claim to love. For example, take the late group called The Revolutionary Workers Headquarters. Their International Women's Day celebration went like this. 1) A welcoming speech 2) Watch Salt of the Earth 3) Sing What Have Women Done? 4) Serve lemonade and cookies pitch for cash 5) Go home. So, let's look at the movie. It was okay the time it was made. However, the film makers only limited the victory of this strike. These film makers can't think of a world where work for wages does not exist. The traditional left looks at creative people as slogan makers and banner painters. For example, the Baltimore chapter of the Workers' World Party has a large lovely looking banner of people of all races and ages engaged in struggle. What are they struggling for? More money and a little loosening of the slave change. Are these workers hoisting red flags? No! They are wearing union hats, and holding union signs. I seriously doubt that a picture of workers going fishing would be on that wall. And I would bet my next paycheck the art of Romarie Bearden would never be seen. Yes, I like art from the Soviet Union and the Cultural Revolution. However, the era of the nice wood cut or bold poster needs to move over and new forms art mount the stage. Now anarchists are even sillier. All art looks look comic book art. And even worse like Japanese cartoon art. Music for the anarchist runs from Woody Guthrie to Punk to who knows. But traditional leftists and anarchists would not be caught dead listing to Albert Ayler, much less than anything so deep as John Cage. Not only that but both the established right and the traditional left and anarchists distain any form of thought that makes people think anything but what is on the agenda of their group/class. Traditional leftists sing the song "Gimmie that old communism/ Gimmie that old communism/gimmie that old communism/It's good enough for me. It was good for Marx and Engels" etc. Anarchist just substitute Bakunin for Marx and Engels. Any thought that people can comprehend more than the party line is just not heard of. My Dead Aunt Virginia who stopped bothering when she bought the collective farm would ask me how I could read all the stuff I read and not keep the correct line. My ex-fiancée said the same thing. One is dead the other is not in my life. However, I am here. And I still think.

Now just what does that have to do with John Cage? Let's look at 4:33. 4:33 is a concept where organized sound is replaced by unorganized or un-recognized. This lasts for four minutes and thirty-three seconds. The participants/audience must now pay attention to the surrounding area they are in. With no sound in an organized form, every squeak is heard. The 4:33 experience lets you daydream and not feel so bad about not paying attention. The 4:33 experience might give the listener a chance to hear voices that can't be heard. If the 4:33 experience were forced upon people who claim to love those that they claim to uphold, things might be better. The human mind has two ears and one mouth as Reverend David Carl Olsen tells us once and a while. The human ears are closer to the brain. That in a metaphysical way means the thought are processed by the brain faster through the ears? Perhaps. Be that as it may, listing more often than speaking is good. And listing with empathy and a scientific world outlook is even better. Listening to go along to get along is wrong. Listening with the idea making collective change is what the world needs now! The 4:33 experience gives those involved in it this chance. Try it yourself. Just listen for 4:33. Go on. Put this polemic down, and just listen.

TIME'S UP!!!!!

Do you know why the powers that be and the official left and the anarchist do not want you to do this? It is as simple as haiku. These seemingly disparate forces do not want you to do what they call goofing

277 | Alan Herbert Rowan Baptiste Barysh, M.E.O.B.

off! They both say this. Goofing off disrupts production/the workers struggle/the revolution or who knows what. The real boss says what have you got to listen to? The traditional left puts on Woody Guthrie that tired reformist/sexist labor anthem Union Maid. Your boss at the anarchist worker own run vegan coffee shop wants you to hop to it, and fetch that hot mocha to that high tipping customer. However, every person revolutionary or otherwise welcomes the chance to goof off. And if there was an anthem for the goofing off between serving the people it would be 4:33. Why not. Anyone can shut their pie holes for 4:33. You don't need a special place to partake in the 4:33 experience. You don't have to play an instrument or sing. All you have to do is listen. Go on do it again.

Nice to see you back again. What did you hear? Call me @ 443-239-5325 any time but the time between 4:33 and 4:33 later. The other thing that 4:33 does is it makes you aware of the passage of time. With nothing to do but listen, you become aware of time. Do not hand me that line about just listening. I am no John Cage purist. I do take a peep at my time peace. Come on paying attention to the passage of time is key to knowing how to use time. Paying attention to time and the passing of time lets you know how to love time. What's wrong with loving time? If you love time you will use it wisely. And using time wisely means the more than occasional time you have to do nothing that the unobservant finds important. Goofing off means you control your life and dreams. And when you stop goofing off or in the words of Bucky Baum get tired of sleeping you can rise up renewed and refreshed with bright new ideas that you and all your goof off comrades can use to conquer the world!

What are you waiting for!

Goof offs of the world Goof off then realize you have nothing to lose but your chains.

Appendix A
Random Quotes about Silence

The Soul Journey with Sarah Moussa

Yesterday at 3:11 AM ·

If you're exhausted, rest.

If you don't feel like starting a new project, don't.

If you don't feel the urge to make something new, just rest in the beauty of the old, the familiar, the known.

If you don't feel like talking, stay silent.

If you're fed up with the news, turn it off.

If you want to postpone something until tomorrow, do it.

If you want to do nothing, let yourself do nothing today.

Feel the fullness of the emptiness, the vastness of the silence, the sheer life in your unproductive moments.

Time does not always need to be filled.

You are enough, simply in your being.

--Jeff Foster

Appendix B

'False Consciousness' actually lies in the chapter "Working Day" by Marx.

"The working day contains the full 24 hours, with the deduction of the few hours of repose without which labor-power absolutely refuses its services again.

Hence it is self-evident that the laborer is nothing else, his whole life through, than labor-power, that therefore all his disposable time is by nature and law labor-time, to be devoted to the self-expansion of capital. Time for education, for intellectual development, for the fulfilling of social functions and for social intercourse, for the free-play of his bodily and mental activity, even the rest time of Sunday." (Marx. Capital, 1990, MEGA: 228 - 299)

> " It is more important to go slow and gain the lessons you need along the journey then to rush the process and arrive at your destination empty."
>
> – *Germany Kent*

Going slow. Waiting. Resting. Letting things be. Allowing. Listening. These are willful acts of passive action that we often label as "doing nothing" when in truth, so much is being done. Like meditation, when we pause, repose, wait, listen and submit, surrendering in conscious allowance, we invite the gifts of the Divine Feminine to flow within us. The key is "consciously".

In every period of rest, there can and should be a conscious surrender within us, allowing it. No regrets, no frets, no should - just quiet presence in the moment with a heart of gratitude for this life, this day, this moment. Conscious surrender occurs when we make that allowance and awareness the center of our being, as opposed to resisting it in our minds with thoughts of what we 'ought' to be doing, or feelings of guilt that we are not doing - wretched and unnecessary disturbers of our inner calm. This is an especially easy year to self-criticize any inactivity, being in the thrum of so much chaos and change.

How many times - be honest - do you really allow, let alone encourage yourself to partake in the simple joy of just doing nothing?

It's important to remember that the ways of the Divine Feminine are yin, which is hallmarked with rest, stillness, and darkness; the word "Yin" originally referred to the shady side of a slope. These spaces are where all true healing and growth occur. It will happen regardless of whether you fret about the seeming lack of action - but how much better to simply surrender and in wisdom than only accept them, it actually experiences the process?

And so, mysterious beloved, I invite you to allow yourself the conscious gift of your stillness today. May your center in the confidence and knowledge of how important your gifts are to this changing world, remembering that you were born for this, and are reading this right now for a reason.

That you are divinely aligned, the womb of creation itself, formed from stars.

(Rest well and deep - and remember)
"Ophelia"
Mixed Media
2017

She Who Is

June 12 at 7:55 AM ·

" It is more important to go slow and gain the lessons you need along the journey then to rush the process and arrive at your destination empty."

– Germany Kent

Appendix C

"There Comes A Time" Tony Williams

Dedicated to the Statue of David by Michelangelo

There comes a time when all that you strive for reaches a peak.

All your dreams must come to the fore!

Everything else in the universe is put on hold for a brief hiatus.

In this pause this absence of organized sound you may hear

A green candle being lit in a Chianti Bottle

The fur of a dog belly being rubbed

The exhale of a museum mummy.

The click of a birch tree.

The sound of a wink or

The sound of heart beats.

Cherish the moment of expiation.

Life will flow in and out of you and you.

Joy will flood your body/bodies

The sound of smile will return to your faces.

You time to shine has arrived here today

Go on and shine

Go ahead look.

Look up!

There's something out there in the universe!

It's a star with your name on it

"Time has come today" The Chambers Brothers

Appendix D

"Relax, Recharge and Reflect

Sometimes it's okay to do nothing!"

Izey Victoria Odaise

The Simplicity Heart

Appendix E

"Time is like a river.

You cannot touch the same water twice

because the flow that has passed will never pass again.

Enjoy every moment of your life"

Anonymous Facebook Post

CHAPTER EIGHT

Musings on Silence

1) Is Silence A Euro-Centric-Concept?

Now dear reader I must ask you to stop and think about what I am asking. Is Silence A Euro-Centric Concept? Now you might be thinking that I must be some kind of Afro-Centric Cultural Nationalist to be raising this question.

Or you might be one of those "official" leftists who only see discussing "relevant" issues like why is the price of gasoline going up again or why we should call prostitutes "sex workers" or some other form of woke balderdash. And have bartered your imagination for a pair of Doc Martin's shoes and therefore cannot possibly conceive of a question like this, because you have the vision of a bat and the hearing ability of a statue. To you I say this; "Official Leftist go pound sand!"

Now for the rest of you who are wondering just what I am asking. Let me start by saying a few words about what I believe are some of the beliefs of the cultures of indigenous people. I have been told that there is a belief among some peoples of indigenous nations that there are spirits in this world who speak to us the living. Now do not get me wrong. This bit of rumination in print is not about spirits, Gods, Goddesses, or anything supernatural. This bit of print pondering is about silence. So, all you what is going on in Area 51 and Chariots of The God's folks have the right to stop reading at this point.

Okay now for the rest of us, I ask the question again. Is Silence A Euro-Centric Concept? For this, we must once again return to the cultures of the Indigenous Peoples. As I have stated before, I have heard that the Indigenous Peoples believed in spirits. You know like the spirit of the land or the spirit of the water. In further but limited observation, I have been led to believe that these same Indigenous Peoples said they could hear these spirits speak to them. If these Indigenous Peoples believed that spirits did in fact speak to them, then that would mean these spirits were speaking to these peoples. Speech means organized sound. Speech means communication. Therefore, while those of you who do not follow John Cage have no real understanding of the idea that silence does not exist outside of a sound-proof room. For those of us who follow John Cage, the concept of non-organized sound is the keystone of the appreciation of sound.

Sound as non-Cage disciples, know it is an organized phenomenon. Music is notes organized into sound. The sound of a car backfiring is an organized sound. The backfiring of an automobile is brief. However, brief it is this sound has a beginning a middle and an end-even though one might not be able to hear all three parts of this organized sound. However, hard as you try will only hear the start and finish of this sound. The middle section of a backfiring of a car merges with the beginning and ending. That would mean to the average listener this sound is continuous. However continuous sounds do have a beginning, a middle, and an end. It's just that most of us do not give a hoot about finding a middle section of say fingernails on a blackboard. We just wish this sound would stop.

Then taking the concept of what is organized and un-organized sound a little further, let us ponder this thought. Are there organized sounds that can only be heard by a few who know what the organizational structure of that sound is? That would mean that a member of a community of Indigenous People can hear messages in what we non-indigenous people call "ambient sounds"? Taking this idea, a bit further could a member of an Indigenous Community be hearing the spirit of a deity when the wind is blowing through the trees? This does not mean that a non-religious person would doubt that the "wind spirit" was trying to communicate with anyone. However, it does mean that the member of this Community of Indigenous People is unaware of the plethora of sounds that can be heard when organized sound yields the podium to unorganized sound. What it does mean is that the rest of the world must understand that as long as there is unorganized sound-there will be sound.

Now let's take this concept further. Let us look at the music of people who live in what is known as "The Third World" as well as the people of the Indigenous Nations of what is known as The United States. The casual listener will hear continuous sounds. When one listens to say the music of the people of the rain forest you will a continuous flow of sounds. That doesn't mean that some of the performers will not stop playing. It does mean however that taken as a whole the music will not stop until the musicians decided it will stop.

Now here is where I am going to go into a bit of conjecture. Let us look at the climate of the Third World and perhaps the climates of the Southern European nations. These climates are warm or even hot climates. Aside from tropical storms most of the sounds are quite pleasant to listen to. You know like the wind in the palm trees, the soft lowing of cows, the pleasant baah of the sheep, the cluck-cluck of chickens, etc. With that in mind, think about this. If the only sounds one usually heard in these climates were sounds that were pleasing to the ear, and if one believed that these sounds were the spirits speaking to you, then wouldn't you want to create sounds so rich and robust that every bit of the non-sounds would be engulfed in joyous music and sounds so as to please the spirits and deities?

Now let's take this one step further. Where do the spiciest foods come from? The Third World is the source of both spices and spicy foods. These foods fill the pallet of the diner much in the same way the joyous music encompasses the non-sounds.

When we look at the countries where "classical music " comes from - we find the sounds of the environment to be less pleasant to listen to. For example(s) the howl of the wind in a blizzard, or the incessant pounding of hailstones. Along with that, you had the industrial noise of the industrial revolution. Naturally, the people of these countries might yearn for silence. This would also include the composers of that time. Could this desire for silence have given the composers of the day to create rests to both give the listening audience and the performers a chance to listen to both the creative organized sound as well as the ambient non-organized sound?

Is There A Class Nature To "Silence"

Or

Is "Silence" Only A Luxury Of The Well-To-Do?

Some will argue that even posing this question is just silly. Let them think that. However, should the more curious of the interested just might about this question. For those who have not let their imaginations and sense of wonder be hijacked by the dull soul -stifling "ideas" of the equally dull and non-revolutionary so-called "left" this thought should provoke thought.

In this light, let us briefly look back at the past. We shall start back with antebellum south. For the slaveowner/master silent slaves were *dangerous* slaves. To these rotten soulless swine, anytime "his" slaves were quiet he thought his "talking tools" were "up to something". And the slaver knew that when his "property" was "up to something" his white ass was in trouble.

This is why when "The Master" was out overseeing his property the slave overseer would holler out "make a noise" or words to that effect when his boss was riding by. Then the slaves would start singing a gospel song. This had the effect of assuaging the quite rightly paranoid slaver that everything was on the up and up. And sadly, when his property was singing it might be that it was then that he should have worried.

That is because what the slaver thought when he heard his slaves singing-he thought they were happy. However, this just might have been untrue. That is because the gospel music of the day also had coded messages. For example, take the phrase "steel away to Jesus" . To the average yokel/slaver it meant going up to heaven to be with Jesus (A.K.A dyeing). However, to the slave it meant something different. It meant getting away or hoping to get away from the plantation. That is because the first slave ship to come to these shores was called **The Good Ship Jesus**. That meant steeling away to Jesus was either going home or getting away. (Rather than go into this further, this author has a whole section dedicated to gospel music in a further part of this tome)

While the southern slaver was trying to make his slaves more vocal, the northern industrialists were making it more difficult for his employees to speak up. With the advent of the Industrial Revolution came the dawn of machines that made noise. With this noise came the lack of silence. With the lack of silence came the lack of a means for conversation between workers. Along with the ever-presence of all that noise was the breakneck speed of the assembly lines that were to be a byproduct of this revolution. Now add to this mix the fact that the forty-hour work was still a dream, both silence and any form of meaningful conversation between workers on the job and workers at home was at best a luxury.

And as time continues the cultural slave masters who control what they want the "masses" call music began to cash in on the importance of flashing lights and loud repetitious "music". What began as rock and roll devolved into disco "music". The disco became a mecca for the work weary soul to go to "unwind" here amid the thump-thump sounds and all the lights and lasers and revolving glass spheres your average disco goer could lose him or her herself in the din and faux excitement of this Huxleyan

Hedonism. It was here sans the soma of The book **Brave New World** was where the disco lizard could unwind and be assured that the highest aspiration one person could have for another could be summed up in the phrase "There's nothing more I'd like to do than take the floor and dance with you"[10]. Once again noise and completive thought were considered an anathema to the Saturday Night Fever Crowd.

When disco had shot it's wad-rap and hip hop came onto the scene. Sadly, what was considered to be a new rebellious music form that **the composer/musician Max Roach** thought had given birth to this generations **Charlie Parkers and Dizzy Gillespie's** degenerated into songs with misogynistic lyrics, sung by rappers who had more ink on them than the Sunday Times, female backup singers who looked like puffed up undulating sex objects and a sanctifying of the "thug Life"

Along with this came the stigma of the silent one-the thoughtful one. Phrases like "navel gazer" or "bump on a log" were used as a put down for those who chose to be more comparative at times. Thinking and reading were (and still are) looked down upon by these people.

However, as this was going on silence was being lauded by the cultural elites. Whole concert Halls, Theaters, Libraries and the like were erected as temples of polite silence. While these areas of polite silence were not officially segregated from those who needed it the most-the stigma of actually enjoying these venues was looked down upon. It also did not help that this stigma was enforced by the so-called "left" who to this very day consider "folk music" to be what workers should listen to.

---

[10] Shake Your Groove Thing -by **Peaches And Herb.**

That is perhaps why the average person on the street eschews any form of music other than what is force fed upon him or her. Do you doubt this author? Okay when was the last time you heard chamber music at a dance club?

Columbo Coda

Does the phrase "Pipe down I can't hear myself **THINK**

"resonate to you?

It should!

Appendix A

Consciousness' actually lies in the chapter "Working Day" by Marx.

"The working day contains the full 24 hours, with the deduction of the few hours of repose without which labor-power absolutely refuses its services again.

Hence it is self-evident that the laborer is nothing else, his whole life through, than labor-power, that therefore all his disposable time is by nature and law labor-time, to be devoted to the self-expansion of capital. Time for education, for intellectual development, for the fulfilling of social functions and for social intercourse, for the free-play of his bodily and mental activity, even the rest time of Sunday." (Marx. Capital, 1990, MEGA: 228 - 299)

" It is more important to go slow and gain the lessons you need along the journey then to rush the process and arrive at your destination empty."

– Germany Kent

Going slow. Waiting. Resting. Letting things be. Allowing. Listening. These are willful acts of passive action that we often label as "doing nothing" when in truth, so much is being done. Like meditation, when we pause, repose, wait, listen and submit, surrendering in conscious allowance, we invite the gifts of the Divine Feminine to flow within us. The key is "consciously".

In every period of rest, there can and should be a conscious surrender within us, allowing it. No regrets, no frets, no should - just quiet presence in the moment with a heart of gratitude for this life, this day, this moment. Conscious surrender occurs when we make that allowance and awareness the center of our being, as opposed to resisting it in our minds with thoughts of what we 'ought' to be doing, or feelings of guilt that we are not doing - wretched and unnecessary disturbers of our inner calm. This is an especially easy year to self-criticize any inactivity, being in the thrum of so much chaos and change.

How many times - be honest - do you really allow, let alone encourage yourself to partake in the simple joy of just doing nothing?

It's important to remember that the ways of the Divine Feminine are yin, which is hallmarked with rest, stillness, and darkness; the word "Yin" originally referred to the shady side of a slope. These spaces are where all true healing and growth occur. It will happen regardless of whether you fret about the seeming lack of action - but how much better to simply surrender and in wisdom than only accept them, it actually experiences the process?

And so, mysterious beloved, I invite you to allow yourself the conscious gift of your stillness today. May your center in the confidence and knowledge of how important your gifts are to this changing world, remembering that you were born for this, and are reading this right now for a reason.

That you are divinely aligned, the womb of creation itself, formed from stars.

(Rest well and deep - and remember)
"Ophelia"
Mixed Media
2017

She Who Is

June 12 at 7:55 AM ·

" It is more important to go slow and gain the lessons you need along the journey then to rush the process and arrive at your destination empty."

– Germany Kent

Why This Writer Finds The Blues And 'False Consciousness' actually lies in the chapter "Working Day" by Marx.

"The working day contains the full 24 hours, with the deduction of the few hours of repose without which labor-power absolutely refuses its services again.

Hence it is self-evident that the laborer is nothing else, his whole life through, than labor-power, that therefore all his disposable time is by nature and law labor-time, to be devoted to the self-expansion of capital.

Time for education, for intellectual development, for the fulfilling of social functions and for social intercourse, for the free-play of his bodily and mental activity, even the rest time of Sunday." (Marx. Capital, 1990, MEGA: 228 - 299)

> " It is more important to go slow and gain the lessons you need along the journey then to rush the process and arrive at your destination empty."
>
> *– Germany Kent*

Going slow. Waiting. Resting. Letting things be. Allowing. Listening. These are willful acts of passive action that we often label as "doing nothing" when in truth, so much is being done. Like meditation, when we pause, repose, wait, listen and submit, surrendering in conscious allowance, we invite the gifts of the Divine Feminine to flow within us. The key is "consciously".

In every period of rest, there can and should be a conscious surrender within us, allowing it. No regrets, no frets, no should - just quiet presence in the moment with a heart of gratitude for this life, this day, this moment. Conscious surrender occurs when we make that allowance and awareness the center of our being, as opposed to resisting it in our minds with thoughts of what we 'ought' to be doing, or feelings of guilt that we are not doing - wretched and unnecessary disturbers of our inner calm. This is an especially easy year to self-criticize any inactivity, being in the thrum of so much chaos and change.

How many times - be honest - do you really allow, let alone encourage yourself to partake in the simple joy of just doing nothing?

It's important to remember that the ways of the Divine Feminine are yin, which is hallmarked with rest, stillness, and darkness; the word "Yin" originally referred to the shady side of a slope. These spaces are where all true healing and growth occur. It will happen regardless of whether you fret about the seeming lack of action - but how much better to simply surrender and in wisdom than only accept them, it actually experiences the process?

And so, mysterious beloved, I invite you to allow yourself the conscious gift of your stillness today. May your center in the confidence and knowledge of how important your gifts are to this changing world, remembering that you were born for this, and are reading this right now for a reason.

That you are divinely aligned, the womb of creation itself, formed from stars.

(Rest well and deep - and remember)
"Ophelia"
Mixed Media
2017

She Who Is

June 12 at 7:55 AM ·

" It is more important to go slow and gain the lessons you need along the journey then to rush the process and arrive at your destination empty."

– Germany Kent

Why This Writer Finds The Blues And Jazz So Amazing

Appendix B
Lee Morgan Sidewinder/Waiting To Answer

Now let us turn our attention to the African American Classical Music (AKA "Jazz" AKA A.A.C.M) composer/trumpet performer/ **Lee Morgan**. In the sixties, **Lee Morgan** was part of a grouping of musicians that recorded on the **Blue Note** label. Along with others on the **Blue Note** label, such as **Herbie Hancock, Lee Morgan** recorded a number of compositions that had for lack of a better word a "funky/jazzy" sound. These compositions such as **Watermelon Man, The Rump Roller and Blind Man Blind Man** all have a definite feel. The themes are what this author would call "Bouncy/Dancy" compositions. To the ears of this listener, they are all based on perhaps one or two chords. If played back- to- back, these compositions would have two reactions. To the neophyte/parvenu/music snob these compositions will soon become boring. However, when the serious listener of A.A.C.M playing these compositions back-to-back a quite subtitle pattern of theme-and variations will become quite self -evident.

While **The Lee Morgan composition Sidewinder** has all of the ear marks of all the rest of these compositions, there is *one* brief singular difference between **The Sidewinder** and these other compositions. The difference is a brief pause of no more than a few seconds between where the written composition ends and the spontaneous composing (AKA

"Soloing) begins. This brief "silent" space/bridge creates a tension that is followed by the spontaneous composing that **Lee Morgan** begins. Thus, in these brief seconds **Lee Morgan** has set his composition **The Sidewinder** apart from all the rest of these compositions. While doing this **Lee Morgan** has set the bar a little higher for his contemporaries. Now instead of launching into a pre-set pattern-the first spontaneous composer must make the beginning of the period allotted to her/him as compelling as possible-in order to keep the listener's attention. And in doing so made this composition more compelling.

What made **Lee Morgan** think of this idea? Who knows. Perhaps-just perhaps it was a former employer of the composer/Trumpet Performer **Dizzy Gillespie?** I the iconic composition **Night In Tunisia,** there is a break between the end of the theme and the beginning of the formal section of improvised composing. In this brief spot the potential soloist must create a brief passage of unaccompanied organized sounds that will tie the written composition to the section of chord structured spontaneous composing. For this author, this brief moments of what could be called anticipatory spontaneous composing will or will not set the tone for the performance. Should the soloist choose by ignorance this will take the edge of the rest of the performance. However, should the soloist come on strong-the whole tenor of the performance will benefit. As it is with **The Sidewinder**, this section of the composition relies on silence to bolster the effort. It's just that obvious.

CHAPTER NINE

Part Two

Why the Blues and Jazz So Doggoned Amazing
Part One The Blues, Jazz, and Revolution.

As readers of The Alan Barysh Facebook of Amazing Stuff already know-this FB page celebrates ALL THINGS AMAZING! This includes people, places, things, foods, clothes, and a whole lot more. This list includes musical forms. These few words are a perfect segue to the reason yours truly wrote this tome.

Ever since a friend of my parents and a local rabbi turned this author on to the blues and Jazz the task of popularizing these music forms has been a real priority in the life of yours truly. Not only has this author had to contend with people who like their music almost as much as they like naked pasta and Miller Light Beer, but this author had to deal with "lefties" who called these musical forms "non -proletarian". Mike Misselman who was expelled from the Revolutionary Communist Party for cheating on his wife while she was pregnant said these musical forms were "sexist"(sic) Jacob Cook who gave up on any form of politics misquoted Mao when he said: "Jazz worships tailing spontaneity". Mao was talking about the self-proclaimed "revolutionary" who sees a political upheaval and blindly follows the "leadership" of these movements behaving like cheerleaders instead of the role these folks should have of uniting with these movements and bringing the people involved in these struggles into the ranks of revolutionary struggle. Mr. Cook who also believed that "After the revolution workers will be able to buy *alligator shoes* "(sic) did not read where Mao said something to the effect that Communism embraces but does not control innovation in all specters of life.

That brings this author to the sixties when Jazz had a more revolutionary appeal to this author than folk music. To this very day listing to Joan Baez sing "All my Sorrows" just doesn't cut it when compared to Nina Simone singing "I Wish I Knew How It Would Feel To Be Free" After shaking off the shackles of trade-unionism this author found that "Four Sisters" by Nina Simone was a more artistic and political statement than "Union Maid" (or about 98% of Woody Guthrie's songs), Should one peruse the titles of a lot of Jazz Compositions one will find such titles as Suite

Mao by Archie Shepp and Max Roach, Freedom Suite by sonny Rollins, Black Brown and Beige by Duke Ellington and the collaborations by Carla Bley and Charlie Haden in the Liberation Music Orchestra both esthetically and politically spot on. Remember Mao has told us that no matter how correct the politics of something is if it stinks artistically it stinks politically.

This is why this writer likes music by The Art Ensemble of Chicago, The musical Jazz and Poetry collaborations of Charles Mingus, Leonard Feather, and Langston Hughes or Ameri Baraka much more palatable than the songs of Prairie Fire or Holly Near. This is also why this author thinks The Internationale should be sung up-tempo and perhaps with better music. This also is why this writer worries that if "respectable lefties" get ahold of state power all forms of culture will be red pablum. These" lefties" forget Mao said "Let a hundred flowers bloom. Let a hundred schools of thought contend" With that said and space running out stay tuned for the next part of this polemic. There Is A Method To What You Call The Madness of The Blues." This will be followed by another polemic "Even Improvisation Has Structure" stay tuned folks.

The Blues Ain't Nothin' But A Good Man (Woman) Feeling Bad

Part One

There Is A Method To The "Madness" Of the Blues
Part A The Musical Structure Of the Blues

Contrary to what some people think, the musical form of the Blues has a musical structure all of its own. The most basic form of the blues is the twelve-bar blues. [11]For the average human who knows little about music- this reporter will go into a little music lesson. All western music is divided into what are called bars. A bar in any form of music is where you write the notes in. As in any musical form, the composer just can't put a zillion notes into just one bar. The number of notes one may put into the bar is determined by what is called the time signature. The time signature is the fraction thing that is at the beginning of a musical composition. To the mind of this composer, the 4/4-time signature is the most common time indicator in the blues. 4/4- time means this. There are four beats to a measure and the quarter note gets the "one beat". What does this mean? Well, all western music has certain divisions of what is called the "whole" not. A "whole note" lasts the full measure of the bar, it is placed in. This "whole note" will last from the beginning of the bar to the end. After the "whole note" there is the "half note" and the "quarter note" and so on down the line. The smaller the time signature the faster the music. That means

---

[11] The Twelve Bar Blues is not the sad feeling one gets after leaving the twelfth bar and still feeling depressed. It is the primary way the Blues is played. This musical form is often pop songs and Jazz compositions also.

4/4 music is this. There are four beats to a bar (or "measure") and the "quarter note" gets the "one" beat.

The chord structure of the blues follows this pattern. In the twelve bars assigned for the blues, the chord structure is 1111/4411/5511. This translates into this. Every form of western music is based on chords. These chords are made up of notes. All chords are made of "triads". A musical "triad " consists of the "root" chord -or the note the chord is based on. The "third" note of the chord progression is three notes above the "root" chord and the "fifth" note is five notes above the root chord. This chord structure also applies to all western forms of music. The "one chord" is the key in the composition is written in. A chord with a note above the "one chord" is called a "second" chord. There are eight notes in the western musical scale. That means the basic blues chord pattern of the blues starts out with four bars of "one" chords for four bars. In the next four bars, you have two "four" chords. These chords are notes based on a note of four steps or places above the "one" chord. The next two notes in the next two notes in the seventh and eighth bar of this song go back to the "one" chord. The ninth and tenth bars of this composition are based on" fifths" meaning the fifth chord is based on a chord five notes above the "one chord". The song is resolved by with two "one chords" making this a twelve-bar blues. The other thing that makes the blues sound the way they do are notes that are called "Blue Notes". We shall discuss this in the next installment.

Part B The Musical Structure Of the Blues

In the previous part of this piece, we learned that in western music all chords have what are known as "triads". You remember the root -the tonic and the fifth. However, the traditional western music chord is made up of four notes. Along with the other component parts of a western music, the chord is the octave. The octave note is the eighth and last note of the western musical scale.

Now that you know a western musical chord is made up of four notes which are the root(or the tonic)the third -and the fifth the next logical question would be this. Why is the last component part of a western musical chord called what it is called?

To answer that question, one must look at the structure of the western musical scale. All traditional western musical scales are either based on the heptatonic seven-note scale or a pentatonic scale. Let's get rid of talking about the pentatonic scale first. The word pentatonic has its' etymologic root in the word pentagon. You know like that building in this nation's capital. The pentagon in Washington DC has five equally distanced sides. These five-sided figures are called a pentagon. Therefore, the adjective for any structure like this is pentatonic. How does this scale sound? When you go to a piano play the first note after the c note. (The middle c note is found in the middle on a piano where there are no black keys between two white keys) By just playing these five notes you have a pentatonic scale. To this writer's ear, this scale has a somewhat mystical sound to it. This mystic sound is a natural feeling to it when a blues guitarist or any other blues musician plays it. (Rather than go into detail just google pentatonic scales to find out more) The other feature of this scale is that the average musical parvenu /blowhard can play anything using the pentatonic scale and have a somewhat interesting sound. If you think that this far- fetched-try it yourself.

For the reader's edification these scales are illustrated below

These are pentatonic scales

*Notes played: C, D, E, G, A

Now see a shape for the A minor pentatonic scale:

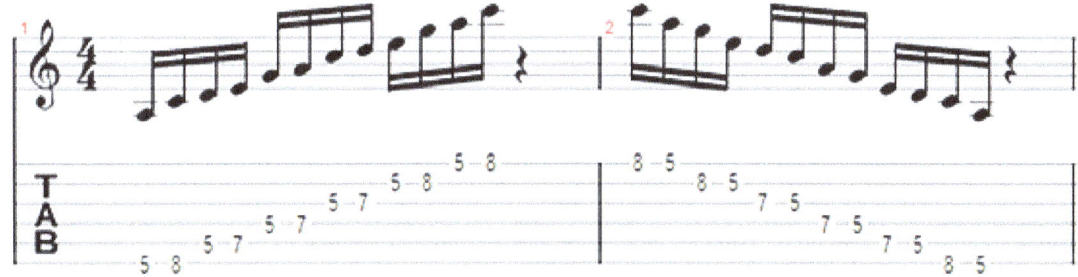

*Notes played: A, C, D, E, G

This is the C Major heptatonic scale.

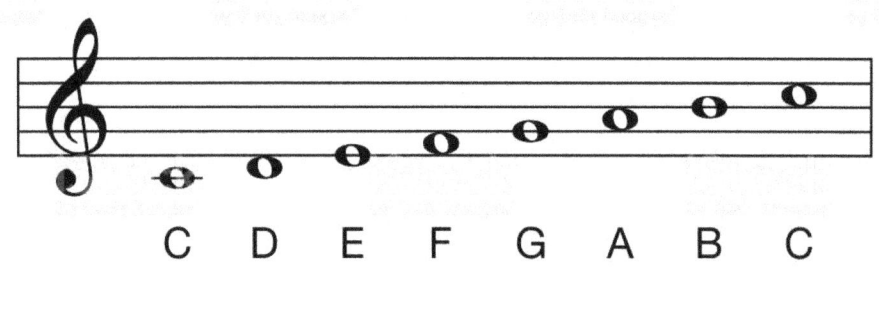

C D E F G A B C

At this point- it would behoove your author to take a break and read something else or play Lilly's Garden on your iPhone.

With that out of the way-let, us turn our attention to the heptatonic scale.

Part C

The Heptatonic Scale, And "Blue Notes"

The heptatonic scale is what most western music is based on. (This author says most western music because the composers Arnold Schonberg and Charles Ives base their music on a twelve-tone scale. Three other composers Lamont Young Harry Partch and Ornette Coleman have also invented non-heptanoic scales. Ornette Colman has created what he calls a "harmolodic" scale. Harry Partch and Lamont Johnson have based their compositions on what they call a "Micro-tonal scale") However, lest this tome is diverted into an essay on European and Western Classical Music it would be best to dwell on our friend the heptatonic scale. The heptatonic scale is based on seven notes. (Some say eight if you include the note after the seventh note that starts the next scale) All major heptatonic scales have the same structure. The structure is built on what are called whole steps, and half steps. This is how they work. The scale is whole step/whole step/half step/whole step/ whole step/whole step/half step. What does this mean? For this, we should look at a keyboard. Let us start at the middle c-the middle key in the piano. Go ahead and play this note. You will find that your favorite scale do-ray-me-fa-so-la-te-do can be played on only the white keys. However, when you play any note after the middle c note you will find out that your major scale falls somewhat short of the mark and in order to make it sound like a regular scale you must include a black key or two. These black keys are the half-steps needed to make the scale sound like a scale. This scale system is part of what is called the "Well-Tempered Scale" or the chromonic scale. This scale has all of the sharps and flats of the eight-note octave scale

With that in mind let us turn our attention to the scales used in Blues and Jazz. The one thing that makes the Blues in Jazz and Blues music sound like they do is the presence of "blue notes" The "blue note" comes when the more traditional non- western scales are forced to "live" in a western musical composition. The result is a clash between western and non - western music. These "blue notes" are used to give a resolution to the music and then create a new musical form. When a musician plays a "blue note" he or she is, in reality, reaching for a note that lies as the composer Leonard Bernstein once said was "somewhere between the cracks in the standard keyboard" It is this clash between traditional western music and other non-western scales that make The Blues and Jazz sound the way they do. This can be heard in the Blues when a guitar or harmonica or bass guitar or any other as well as a good vocalist. For the purposes of brevity, we will look at and the guitar and the harmonica. When the guitarist looks like he or she is pushing a string of the guitar one way or another you hear what is called a "bent note" or a "blue note". When the harmonica player bends the harmonica one way or another these "bent notes" or "blue notes" make the blues sound like the blues.

This brings us to what should be obvious to anyone with ears. The music of the Blues is a bone fide musical form. And along with the space left out for "open blowing" is a form of classical music. What do you doubt this writer? Well, this is just the time for you to 86 all of your western chauvinism. Just like a fugue or a symphony-the Blues has a basic musical structure that must be strictly adhered to lest it not be the Blues. Just as a symphony must have five distinct parts-so the Blues must have a set chord and note pattern to be the Blues. It matters not that there is room for spontaneous composition or what some parvenu might call improvising. If the soloist does not spontaneously create within the form and structure of the blues-it just ain't the blues. To be as William S. Burroughs would say "Country simple" just because Bach did not compose The Backwater Blues does not mean this composition isn't classical music of a different type. Do you disagree? Then you most likely will run to your medicine cabinet for some Excedrin when you find out Rag Time Music is also considered classical music. Why is this? That is because Rag Time Music must follow a certain set of musical protocols to be called Rag Time Music. And not only that but all Rag Time Music was written out entirely. Along with that-before the dawn of recorded music-Rag Time Music could only be heard by the composer or by purchasing the sheet music and performing it at home.

When looking at what western musical chauvinists call "classical music" the only classical music-one ignores the classical music of a lot of non-western countries. For example, the raga of Indian music or the throat singing of the Tibetan people, or Gamelan music of the Indonesian people all fit quite well into the definition of classical music. And to be seven more specific all "folk music" is really people's classical music. This author will let you in the words of the poet Marcus Colasurdo "put it in your brainpan and fry it up a bit" While you are cooking in the kitchen-this might be a good place to take a break. In the next installment we will look into why the Blues is a form of poetry just like the sonnet or haiku.[12]

---

[12] In passing this author feels it would behoove you dear reader to know about other scales than the **Major scale.** The **Minor Scale is a major scale with a lowered 7th and 3rd.** The **Dominant Scale is a Major Scale with a lowered 7th.** And just to make sure you know what a **Blues scale is it is like the Minor scale without the 2nd.** The rest of a **Blues scale continues with this omission but a flat fifth is added and a natural 5th and no 6th note.** This scale looks like this three whole steps are followed by two half steps three whole steps

Part D

The Blues Is Poetry Set To Music

Aside from what people call "free verse" in which each poem has a logic and meter all of its own, every poem has a structure. For example, the Japanese Haiku has a distinct form. The Haiku consists of three lines of poetry. The first line is five syllables. The second line is seven syllables long. The third line is five syllables long. (Note your author said syllables, not words) . The sonnet has a structure that for reasons of brevity we shall mention only in passing we shall not delve into. The Blues has a structure all of its' own. The poet Langston Hughes describes it in the words your author will paraphrase. Every Blues poem has four lines of poetry written in the iambic pentameter form.

Iambic poetry is like a "walking poem" because it has rhythm that imitates the way most folks walk. That rhythm is right/LEFT/right/LEFT/right/LEFT and so on. The walking gate is achieved by putting the beat of the poem on every second beat of the poem. If you try reciting the lyrics of a Blues song while walking you will get the point your author is trying to make.

There are four couplets in a Blues composition. This is where your author takes issue with Langston Hughes who says there are three lines in the poem. Mr. Hughes says the first two lines of a Blues composition are in fact one long repeated line broken into two parts. Your author must side with the poet Ameri Baraka who says the first two lines are in fact a couplet.

Okay with this "tempest in a teapot" argument aired and put aside let's look at the structure of a Blues composition. The second line of a Blues composition just echoes the first line. The third line is a non-rhyming line or a transitional line. The fourth line has a word that ties up these couplets with a rhyming word that rhymes with the first two couplets. This line also completes the poem. This line also is the resolution of each stanza. This line is where for lack of a better word is where irony or "punch line" is contained

Take these examples of a Blues stanza

> "Please mister foreman won't you slow this assembly line
> Please mister foreman won't you slow this assembly line
> 'Cause I don't mind workin'
> But I really don't like dyin' "

Or

> "Talk about your woman I wish you could see mine
> Talk about your woman I wish you could see mine
> The way she looks
> Could bring eyesight to the blind

Any deviation in this structure means the effort is not a Blues stanza. Not even if you are the reincarnation of Ogden Nash. This structure in both music and lyrics belies the puffed-up know-it-alls who think that the Blues are just "folk music"

Probably the other reason these poems are downplayed by poetry snobs is because of the subject manor. To put it in a nutshell the Blues are a reflection of the life and times and even hard times Black people have faced and still face. The Blues is all about suffering, and hard times. But the Blues is also about good times and love both requited and unrequited love. The Blues is about the daily grind and the good times life has given us. **Bob Avakian** the revolutionary leader noted that it is truly amazing that something as beautiful as the music and culture that has been created despite the centuries of brutal oppression reigned down upon them. This is also why listening to the Blues will strike a resonating chord with all people who have known the joys and sufferings of life. As a line of a Blues song goes "If you've ever been mistreated then you know what I'm talking about." That is why a white-middle-class Jewish kid named **Mike Bloomfield** can relate to the Blues. History tells us of "the Children of Israel" laboring under the whip of the Pharoah-just as the kidnaped African slaves did in the pre-civil war south. And think about this -the word Ghetto as applied to a neighborhood was where the Jews of Europe were forced to live.-just like the Ghettos of today. Both Black people and Jewish people have had their own holocausts. Both Black people and Jews are considered inferior people by bigots of all types. And on the upscale side, Both Black people know just how to get down and party as well as stand up for justice no matter who is being put down. Yes, the Blues is the music of life. It is the music of joy and sorrow. With one foot planted in the music of Africa and the other planted in the Gospel Sanctified Sounds of the Amen Corner, the Blues has flourished to become the root source of Jazz/Rhythm and Blues/Soul Music and literally any form of music those without hope can create to give them hope. As Ameri Baraka opined -you can go anywhere in the world and find two things Chinese food and Black music. That's why your author will tell you this is amazing stuff and you better pick up on what's being put down Square Bizz

PS Wait until you get hip to Jazz and why this author thinks this music is amazing

Why Your Facebook Honcho Thinks "Jazz" Should Be Called African-American Classical Music, And Why He Thinks This Music Is Amazing

Part A

Why Should We Call Jazz African-American Classical Music

In order to more fully understand why this writer believes "Jazz" should be called African-American Classical music, this writer would like you to join him as we go down memory lane. The first time your author heard this phrase was when he was attending a **Rassan Roland Kirk** performance at **The Famous Ball Room on 1717 North Charles Street in Baltimore Maryland**

Now just for all of you "out of towners" this author thinks it would behoove him to tell you just a bit about **The Famous Ball Room on 1717 North Charles Street in Baltimore Maryland.** For anyone's money, **The Famous Ball Room on 1717 North Charles Street in Baltimore Maryland** was for this writer the utmost hippest , coolest venue for the "Jazz" aficionado. This place was so hip and funky that it made **Smalls Paradise** look like **Carnegie Hall** Uh-huh that's the gospel truth. This was the place where people from all streams of life went to make friends-eat good food-and enjoy good music. This was the place to hear the music that was more than the soundtrack of your life. This was the place where you could hear music that was the heartbeat of your life. For five dollars you could eat the best soul food, drink the coolest soda, and not only hear the music your inner hipster so longed for, but mix and mingle with the performers. This was the place where "old heads" and young hippies who just got the message **Art Blakey** was sending out. The "kids" from **The Maryland Institute College of Art** could rub shoulders with folks from **Turners Station** just back from church or **Sparrows Point Shipyard Workers** relaxing from the weekend and ready to make it back to the gig on Monday.

And so, on this auspicious day in the summer of "I can't recall" your reporter was at **The Famous Ball Room on 1717 North Charles Street in Baltimore Maryland** listening to **Rassan Roland Kirk**. After this amazing musician made an introduction that went something like this: Thank you, ladies and gentlemen. Our band has just finished a world tour. We performed for the crowned heads of Europe, the potheads of San Francisco, the acid heads of Los Angles, and now we are performing for the wine heads of Baltimore" after that he launched into his composition **Rip Rig And Panic** this was a sure enough, smoking song. However, it was not smoking enough for one listener who yelled out "quit Jivin' and play some African -American Classical Music" In response **Rassan Roland Kirk and company** performed **Take The A Train** and that was the only song that was played for the rest of that hour-long set. (Note **The Famous Ball Room on 1717 North Charles Street in Baltimore Maryland** was known as a place where you could yell stuff like that out to a performer and the performer(s) would take it in good stride. "Give the drummer some" or "Give the bass a taste" were often heard as a sort of mantra. Once when the trumpeter /flugelhornist/vocalist **Clark Terry** was there almost all the people there yelled **Mumbles-Mumbles** his signature vocal composition until he performed it. It was also at this performance where **Clark Terry** sang **I Want A Little Girl** and an oh-so-beautiful young woman yelled out

"You don't need a little girl you need a nurse" This author thinks you get the drift.

Let's roll the clock forward. Your writer was working for what was called **Rowley-Scheer** delivering blueprints. While going from here to there-the radio presented an interview with the composer/artist and "Jazz Musician **Miles Davis**. After the host said a few snarky remarks **Miles Davis** said that the music we call "Jazz" should be called African - American Classical Music and then went on to say why.

At this point, your reporter must pause. Why? This post is already getting too long for Facebook. However, should some magazine publisher wish to publish the full essay about The Blues and Jazz wait until it's all laid out and e-mail Magoo1917@ earthlink.net and we can talk turkey.

Why Jazz is Really African American Classical Music
Part A Continued

From the onset, the interview with **Miles Davis** did not bode well. The very first words out of this kid's mouth were about how difficult it was to arrange the interview. That rubbed **Miles Davis** the worst of the wrong ways. The kid talked about "Jazz Music"(Sic). Well, **Miles Davis** went out on a tangent that was so brilliant the author of this piece thought his radio would start glowing. In that gravelly voice that **Miles Davis** was so well-known for this compose first decried the term "Jazz Music" This great man pointed out how putting the word "Jazz" in front of the word made it look secondary to real music. Like "folk" music. He then said that Jazz should be called **African American Classical Music**. This brilliant musician and composer opined that even though Jazz in this country had some rough and tumble beginnings it still has a form and structure all of its own just like any other type of music.

And low all through all these many-long years, this idea has been ruminating in what the poet **Marcus Colasurdo** would call my "brainpan". And yes low and behold your writer believes that too. For starters let's look at the origin of Jazz.

Many a long and windy essay has been written about both the humble and the brothel birthplaces of Jazz. To spare the reader's time suffice it to say Jazz as a music form came to this country in the form of African music. Somewhere and sometime long ago this African-based music merged with other strains of music to become the music we call Jazz. And to be fair to all the people who say this kind of music or that kind of music was also influential in creating Jazz the basic truth is Jazz is an African based music. Or As the multi-instrumentalist /composer **Pharoah Sanders** said in the title of a composition "Our Roots began in Africa" **Archie Shepp** the multi-instrumentalist and composer put it in a few sentences on the linear note to **Mamma Too Tight**. He said if people can acknowledge and celebrate the ethnic roots of pizza and egg rolls it should be obvious that any aware person should be aware and celebrate the beautiful contributions Africa has given the world. And among the many contributions, Africa has given the world is the tiny musical mustard seed that would take root in the Louisiana city of New Orleans. Then after sinking its roots in the rich Big Easy soil the tree shot up and became the Tree Of Jazz. And this music began to grow to become the various and sundry forms of Jazz.

But wait some people say don't Jazz musicians play popular music. The answer is obviously they do. Did not **Beethoven** incorporate local music in his compositions? That also goes true for **Aaron Copland** and **Charles Ives** also do this. In these compositions the phrase theme and variations is used. Why can't the idea of theme and variation be used when Jazz composers or a single Jazz Composer perform a Jazz, Standard? You have the opening basically an A B A song that is performed. (Note the A B A structure of a song refers to the three distinct sections of a pop song or a Jazz standard. In the first A section of the song, the melody is played. This is followed by a section of music that will tie the first A to the second A. This section is the B section or the bridge. This song has a basic structure and it would defiantly behoove the Jazz composer to abide by them (Unless they are playing "outside the changes" there will more on that. However, even in performing what are called "standards" or original compositions, the form is basically performing the music first and then having a round Robbin of selected improvised or spontaneously composed music (or "solos") this might be followed by an interlude of **Trading Fours** This serious of musical dialogue is called **Trading Fours** for this reason. As you know the basic section of all Western music is the bar. The idea goes like this one composer will play a little four-bar snippet of music. Then another musician replies with a four-line snippet and so on until there is the deliriously wonderful and truly amazing musical special of seeing just how well each musician put their bars into the mix of this musical montage. And should the music reach a point of high energy where two or more musicians are performing or "blowing/cooking" or whatever this becomes a "cutting contest" where each musician tries to be better than the last or "cut" the musician. And should this passionate and eager musical conversation/composition reach a boiling point well-we- "give the drummer some". Or for those of you in Rio Linda the drummer gets a chance to "work his/her chops" or show the audience how this musician can create spontaneous music for solo percussion instruments. Now doesn't that sound better than "drum solo"?

Now let's look back and see why "Jazz Music " is classical music. In all forms of music, some strict rules and protocols must be followed to make this music become classical. Or rather Western classical. The Symphony has five distinct sections. The Fugue and the Cannon also have their own forms, The classical Asian Indian raga has its own form as does the round song. Jazz and Jazz Compositions all have distinct forms also. We have seen the pop music form. However, when they're original Jazz compositions that include improvisation in the mix why isn't this form of music that has a long and cherished history? And if twelve-tone and pan-tonal music is called classical music-then why not Jazz? Could this be because the stigma of anyone not being a dead European man is not "serious music"? It may well could be. You go think about it while this writer gets to work telling you about the wonder of improvised African American Classical music and improvised music

CHAPTER TEN

Part B

Jazz Is The Sounds Of Surprise
OR
On Improvising And Other Spin-Off Ideas

"Listen"
Title from the one-word poem Jazz by Jon Hendricks

"Jazz is the sound of surprise"
Whitney Ballet

Of all the exhilarating forms of music African -American Classical Music (A-A-C-M-is this author's favorite type. However, in all the most reflective and contemplative of this music, this author also finds that A-A-C-M-is at the head of this list. The answer should be obvious to anyone who listens to any form of music with perhaps ambient music or twelve-tone music-to this listener's ears music contains and expresses all forms of feeling and emotion. And should you include a meditative mood then even twelve-tone and ambient music has a less (No way less) some sort of mood. That is should one wish to spend an exhilarating afternoon watching the grass grow you look for a human feeling in the music.

To this listener's ears the sentence "Jazz is the sound of surprise." rings true. Let us look at some examples of the sounds of the sound of surprise in up-tempo music. Lately, your reporter has been listing to quite a bit of sound surprises performed by wind artists. Let's see how many we can put into this segment

SUBSET ONE

THE SOUND OF SURPRISE IN DIRECTED JAZZ

1) Before we venture on this author would like to briefly explain what the phrase "Directed Jazz" means. Directed Jazz is any form of this music that is built around any form either standard or created for this one composition or may compositions either related or unrelated.

For example, the popular song **I've Only Have Eyes For You** follows the typical a-b-a pop song form. **Freedom Suite** by **Sonny Rollins** has the form of the western classical music form the suite.

As with any form of music A-A-C-M has its' exhilarating and its reflective forms of music as well as its' own original music.

SUBSET ONE A

THE SOUND OF SURPRISE IN EXHILARATING AFRICAN-AMERICAN CLASSICAL MUSIC

Sunset A-1)

THE SOUND OF SURPRISE IN ORGANIZED MUSICAL FORMS

Diminuendo and Crescendo In Blue, from the recording Duke Ellington, did at Newport in1967 is a perfect example This elaborately and elegantly arranged orchestral masterpiece features the composer/tenor saxophonist **Paul Gonsalves**. For this listener, this heady solo begins on a rather lackluster solo that builds into a dizzying example of something being convoluting and amazing. Just listen to the twists and turns and variations on a theme that come pouring and leaping out of the bell out of the bell of **Tenor Saxophonist/Composer Paul Gonsalves** will make your head spin.

Down By The Riverside as performed by the recording Oliver Nelson live in Los Angles is another fine example of surprising music in an up-tempo. From the first note of the first trumpet performer/composer to the credit **Composer/arranger/ multi-instrumentalist Oliver Nelson** gives at the end this is a cooking /cutting session that always leaves and hopefully will leave you the listener amazed

The composition **No Private Income Blues by Charles Mingus on the album called Mingus Wonderland** fits the bill. **Booker Ervin** one of the finest and most underrated tenor saxophonists/composers comes on just a whaling and wolf ticket selling as if tomorrow was going to cancel him out. **Booker Ervin** just cooks as if your local rib joint was on top of a volcano. This is one bad -no killer solo. This is a gauntlet-throwing solo that says: "okay chump make my day". After that **Richard Wyands** does a well-crafted abet laid-back that is the equivalent of the sherbet portion of a big Italian dinner. But Hold on folks here comes **John Handy on Alto Saxophone**. Folks, it looks like he is faltering a bit. But wait he's picking up speed. Now hold on folks here comes **Booker Ervin.** What's going on? These cats are trading fours now its notes. This is one killer cutting session When **Ella Fitzgerald** sings **How High The Moon on the recording Mack the Knife Ella in Berlin** if your mind isn't blown to quote **Composer/songwriter/ musician and saxophonist Louis Jordan "Jack you're dead".** This performance is so amazing and full of surprises that even to this very day, your reporter is amazed that this performance gets completed. The song **Everybody's Boppin' from the album The Hottest New Group In Jazz by Lamber Hendricks and Ross is** more breathless than any relative of Jerry Lee Lewis could. This is another song that leaves your reporter gasping and saying: "Gee how did they finish that?" Stay tuned for the next section. The sound of surprise is everywhere, no matter the tempo or amount of people.

Section- B 1)

Surprises Come In All Tempos

In this author's not most humble opinion, there are a lot of folks who take being amazed by listening to music that is bombastic and loud and celebratory. However, there is a whole lot of oogabs of time where the understated or the well-crafted or the substructural nature of the event/creation has the power to make something shiver in the spine.

This author must concede that when **Pianist Keith Jarret** performs his solos on both versions of **Forrest Flower (Forrest Flower and Forrest Flower '69)** his solos are even more intriguing than those of the rest of this quartet. This preference for the soloing of **Keith Jarrett** is best pointed out in the last solo on **Forrest Flower 69**. In this solo **Keith Jarrett** takes the listener on an express ride that traces the roots of Jazz through **Calypso** to **Gospel** to the **Gospel influenced Jazz of Keith Jarrett.**

However, to paraphrase **John Lennon** amazement happens when you're planning something else. In that light, this author is as amazed by **Peace Piece by Bill Evans** as he is by **Gymnopeide by Eric Sate.** The **Trombone performance by Quinten Jackson on the Charles Mingus Composition or the dialogue by Eric Dolphy and Charles Mingus on What Love** is amazing. And with the last composition, this reviewer finds the whole composition **What Love-which is based on the chord changes of What Is This Thing**

Called Love quite kaleidoscopic. **The bass clarinet /Contrabass solo with Charles Mingus is the height of an intense fifteen minutes.** In both the **Quinten Jackson** and the **Mingus/Dolphy duets** the emphasis is on giving the instruments involved a human vocal sound. Rather than go into detail and tell you dear reader how **Quinten Jackson makes his trombone sound like the cry of people in sorrow and Charles Mingus and Eric Dolphy create the sound of two people in an argument** this reviewer will tell you to check these recordings out. Yes check these recordings and be amazed.

However just as you will be amazed by **Billie Holliday singing OOH What A Little Moonlight Can Do For You or Strange Fruit or Gloomy Sunday** and it isn't the tempo of the music that will amaze you.

Let us look at the amazing quality of these three **Billie Holliday recordings**

OOH, What A Little Moonlight Can Do For You Lady Day sings a little homage to the aphrodisiacal qualities that people in love feel while under that Seattleite planet of this planet.

Strange Fruit[13] the song written by Abe Meerpool (AKA Lewis Allen) This is a mournful dirge for yet another murder of yet another Black man. This is still one of the best protest songs ever written in this reviewer's somewhat knowledgeable opinion

Gloomy Sunday should bum you out even worse than **Strange Fruit.** This even more somber song has a strange history. This urban/folk legend

---

[13] A lot of know -it all -but don't Jazz lovers would falsely claim that **Billie Holliday** wrote this song. However, it was written by **Abe Meerpool (AKA Lewis Allen)** who is related to the **Rosenberg's** two activists framed for "stealing government secrets". At the time Abe Meerpool wrote this song he was temporarily in the orbit of the **William Z Foster** cabal of revisionists. (AKA THE "Communist Party")

this writer has heard that **Gloomy Sunday** was released around the time of the **1929 Stock Market Crash.** The story goes on to say that the recording country that **Billie Holliday** was contracted to demand that she put a "happy ending" to this composition. The reason this demand was forced upon this singer was simple. According to this story, either way, too many big-time capitalists or way too few members of the bourgeoisie [14]were jumping out of hotel windows after allegedly being inspired by the song **Gloomy Sunday**

Both mood and texture of a composition are not the prime thing that makes both Blues and Jazz (and other music forms). The heart and soul of the amazement of these music forms is improvisation of all types, We will get into that later on. Subset B On Improvising

---

[14] This summation of these people depends on your world outlook.

Section A-1

On Improvising From Playing The Changes

To Playing The Scales And Modes

Surprises Come In All Tempos

In this author's not most humble opinion, there are a lot of folks who take being amazed by listening to music that is bombastic and loud and celebratory. However, there is a whole lot of oogabs of time where the understated or the well-crafted or the substructural nature of the event/creation has the power to make something shiver in the spine.

This author must concede that when **Pianist Keith Jarret** performs his solos on both versions of **Forrest Flower (Forrest Flower and Forrest Flower '69)** his solos are even more intriguing than those of the rest of this quartet. This preference for the soloing of **Keith Jarrett** is best pointed out in the last solo on **Forrest Flower 69**. In this solo **Keith Jarrett** takes the listener on an express ride that traces the roots of Jazz through **Calypso** to **Gospel** to the **Gospel influenced Jazz of Keith Jarrett.**

However, to paraphrase **John Lennon** amazement happens when you're planning something else. In that light, this author is as amazed by **Peace Piece by Bill Evans** as he is by **Gymnopeide by Eric Sate.** The **Trombone performance by Quinten Jackson on the Charles Mingus Composition or** the dialogue by Eric Dolphy and Charles Mingus on What Love is amazing. And with the last composition, this reviewer finds the whole composition What Love-which is based on the chord changes of What Is This Thing Called Love quite kaleidoscopic. The bass clarinet /Contrabass solo with Charles Mingus is the height of an intense fifteen minutes. In both the Quinten Jackson and the Mingus/Dolphy duets the emphasis is on giving the instruments involved a human vocal sound. Rather than go into detail and tell you dear reader how Quinten Jackson makes his trombone sound like the cry of people in sorrow on the recording Black Saint And The Sinner Lady On Impulse! records. Then listen to What Love on the Charles Mingus recording Mingus Presents Mingus on the Candid Label. On this cut Charles Mingus and Eric Dolphy create the sound of two people in an argument. This reviewer will tell you to check these recordings out. Yes check these recordings and be amazed.

However just as you will be amazed by Billie Holliday singing OOH What A Little Moonlight Can Do For You or Strange Fruit or Gloomy Sunday and it isn't the tempo of the music that will amaze you.

Let us look at the amazing quality of these three Billie Holliday recordings

OOH, What A Little Moonlight Can Do For You Lady Day sings a little homage to the aphrodisiacal qualities that people in love feel while under that Seattleite planet of this planet.

Strange Fruit[15] the song written by Abe Meerpool (AKA Lewis Allen)This is a mournful dirge for yet another murder of yet another Black

---

[15] A lot of know -it all -but don't Jazz lovers would falsely claim that **Billie Holliday** wrote this song. However, it was written by **Abe Meerpool (AKA Lewis Allen)** who is related to the **Rosenberg's two activists framed for**

man. This is still one of the best protest songs ever written in this reviewer's somewhat knowledgeable opinion

Gloomy Sunday should bum you out even worse than **Strange Fruit**. This even more somber song has a strange history. This urban/folk legend this writer has heard that **Gloomy Sunday** was released around the time of the **1929 Stock Market Crash.** The story goes on to say that the recording country that **Billie Holliday** was contracted to demand that she put a "happy ending" to this composition. The reason this demand was forced upon this singer was simple. According to this story, either way, too many big-time capitalists or way too few members of the bourgeoisie [16]were jumping out of hotel windows after allegedly being inspired by the song **Gloomy Sunday**

Both mood and texture of a composition are not the prime things that make both Blues and Jazz (and other music forms). The heart and soul of the amazement of these music forms is improvisation of all types, We will get into that later on. In both the Blues and Jazz, the use of improvisation is what a lot of musicians/composers might call the "meat and potatoes" of these musical forms. However, contrary to what know-nothing do not know about these musical feats in the Blues and Jazz improvisation is always based on something. If we proceed from this notion that even in the most "out there" example of spontaneous composition there is a structure. Let's take a look at one of the most "out there" musical compositions. The choice for today is **Assentation by John Coltrane.** At first, listen the listener hears only what is perceived as chaos. However, upon years of repeated

---

"stealing government secrets". At the time Abe Meerpool wrote this song he was temporarily in the orbit of the William Z Foster cabal of revisionists. (AKA THE "Communist Party")

[16] This summation of these people depends on your world outlook.

listening (both digitally enhanced and the original analog treatments), your reviewer has found a definite pattern in this monumental work.

The recording starts out with a theme. Yes, it's a short theme. However, it is a theme. While the theme is being played the other horn players play what are known in **Dixie Land Jazz** as "passing tones", To the unschooled these "passing tones" are the pleasant embellishments one hears on your run-of-the-mill **New Orleans Brass Band** recordings. However, even if these "embellishments" are "passing tones". Though "a - tonal" in the listener's ear. These notes actually are based on the notes, scales, and modes In a bit we will investigate **Assentation by John Coltrane** However before we go any further it cannot be overstated enough improvisation-no -skillful well performed, and constructed are the key to performing the music The rule both the Blues and Jazz the use of improvisation is what a lot of musician/composers might call the "meat and potatoes" of these musical forms.

However, contrary to what know-nothing do not know about these musical feats in the Blues and Jazz improvisation is always based on something. If we proceed from this notion that even in the most "out there" example of spontaneous composition there is a structure. Let's take a look at one of the most "out there" musical compositions. The choice for today is **Assentation by John Coltrane.** As stated earlier The choice for today is **Assentation by John Coltrane.** At first, listen the listener hears only what is perceived as chaos. However, upon years of repeated listening (both digitally enhanced and the original analog treatments), your reviewer has found a definite pattern in this monumental work.

Then you hear the theme. It's a short one but it's there. Then emerging out of this swirl of theme and "passing tones" comes **John Coltrane.** After a few notes, **John Coltrane** then starts his solo. Upon completion of his solo, **John Coltrane** sort of does a musical backstep exit into the maelstrom. The music continues. Then out of this heady whirlpool comes the next soloist Trumpeter/composer **Dewey Johnson** Who follows the lead of **John Coltrane**. This continues until all the horn players have made their contributions/ Then **McCoy** Tyner *solos and yes his solo is based on the composition!* This is a not-too-subtle way of **John Coltrane** showing the world there was a sense and purpose to his music. (This becomes obvious in the recording **Meditations** where both sides of this recording where Pianist **Mccoy Tyner** takes these compositions out on a mediative tone that perhaps is also based on the structure of these compositions) However in **Assentation**, the ending just winds down with **Percussionist/Drummer/Composer/Elvin Jones** having the last word. So just like all Jazz Compositions this extended work begins with its own logic and schedule and ends just that way.

Now let us look at a standard that gave **John Coltrane** his "go-to" composition for almost all of his life. The composition is The **Rogers and Hammerstein's My Favorite Things from The Sound of Music**.

Section B-2

No, you haven't lost your mind. The statement Now let us look at a standard that gave **John Coltrane** his "go-to" composition for almost all of his life. The composition is The **Rogers and Hammerstein's My Favorite Things from The Sound of Music**. Has been requoted here.

The Atlantic Record of The Rogers and Hammerstein's My Favorite Things from The Sound of Music. (A.K.A "MFT" from now on) It was recorded sometime in March 1961. Shortly before **John Coltrane** left the ensemble of **Miles Davis,** his employer gave him a soprano saxophone. **John Coltrane** did use it in some performances. How in March 1961 **John Coltrane** released **MFT"** for **Atlantic Records**

Until **John Coltrane** chose to use this straight saxophone few if any had performed on it. The saxophone giants **Sidney Bechet and Steve Lacy** performed with this instrument. This seems as though there would be a 189-degree separation between these two men. However, if you remember this writer telling you what "passing tones are" the listener will understand why both a "traditional Jazz " musician and an "Avant Guarde" Jazz saxophonist would choose this instrument as a vehicle to express their musical ideas. (This topic should be gone into in further writings-but not now)

Wikipedia describes the musical soul of **MFT** this way The title track is a modal rendition of the <u>Rodgers and Hammerstein</u> song "My Favorite Things" from <u>*The Sound of Music*</u>. The melody is heard numerous times throughout, but instead of playing solos over the written <u>chord changes</u>, both Tyner and Coltrane take extended solos over <u>vamps</u> of the two <u>tonic</u> chords, <u>E minor</u> and <u>E major</u> (whereas the original resolves to <u>G major</u>),[8] played in <u>waltz time</u>.[9] In the documentary *The World According to John Coltrane*, narrator Ed Wheeler remarks on the impact that this song's popularity had on Coltrane's career:

In 1960, Coltrane left Miles [Davis] and formed his own quartet to further explore modal playing, freer directions, and a growing Indian influence. They transformed "My Favorite Things", the cheerful populist song from 'The Sound of Music,' into a hypnotic eastern <u>dervish</u> dance. The recording was a hit and became Coltrane's most requested tune—and a bridge to broad public acceptance.

This reporter will now describe his first impressions of listing to **MFT**. While relaxing at the Sheppard and Enoch Pratt and getting himself clean and drug-free, he borrowed a copy of **MFT** from a friend. This was not the first time your reporter had seen or heard this recording. However, when first hearing this recording-he did not grasp the innovations on this recording. However, when putting this record on his record player he was immediately enthralled by the oboe-like sound of the soprano saxophone. After stating the theme **Pianist/Composer McCoy Tyner** performs one of the most lyrical performances this writer has had the pleasure of listing to. Listening and re-listening to this performance visions of country streams, sun flowered fresh fields, and hints of **Debussy** as well as a preview of music by **composer/multi-instrumentalist Keith Jarrett,** (To be specific his **Kohn Concert recording on ECM records.** At this point, your writer must take serious issue with **Ameri Baraka** who describes the piano solo as "veers dangerously close to cocktail music" (sic) This author knows that **pianist/composer McCoy Tyner** did not veer close to anything on this composition. **pianist/composer McCoy Tyner** invades the realm of "cocktail music. After liberating all the notes from behind the bars, this pianist/composer sets these former "captive notes" free. Once released from both their 4/4 and show tune restrictions, this young pianist/composer weave's a beautiful solo that paves the way for **John Coltrane**.

With just a few block chords(Chords performed with both hands) **John Coltrane** launches into a muscular, and sinewy solo which is another reason so many people love this composition. Another reason this version of **MFT** is so intriguing is that **The multi-instrumentalist/composer John Coltrane** avoids improvising on the basic chord changes of this show tune. Instead, the song is based on the tonic chords that are played like a two-chord vamp. And in two strokes this hum-drum song has been transformed into something amazing[17]

My Favorite Things from The Sound of Music was recorded in October 1960 for **Atlantic Records**

It features

- **Steve Davis -Bass**
- **Elvin Jones-Drums**
- **McCoy Tyner-piano**
- **John Coltrane-Soprano Saxophone and Tenor Saxophone on other compositions.**

---

[17] For a few examples of a composer/Jazz music check out the article by the **Composer/French horn player Gunther Schuler** on **Sonny Rollins** and thematic improvisation available somewhere on the net. **Mr. Schuler** does a review of the music created by **multi-instrumentalist/composer Sonny Rollins**, and shows the listener the uniqueness of the improvisational work **sonny Rollins** Has done to keep the attention of the listener. For example, **Mr. Rollins** has taken Broadway show tunes like **"Till there Was You"** or**"I'm An Old Cowhand"** and made something wonderful with the notes. **Way Out West on the Contemporary Label** has I'm an Old Cowhand on it. **"Till there was you can be found on the Freedom Suite by Mr. Rollins on the Riverside Label.**

B 3

As Whitney Balliett said: "Jazz is the sound of surprise". This statement can't be overstated. This also can apply to the Blues. Just think about this. When the run-of-the-mill Jazz or Blues lover hears a studio recording and like a particular song-this person will more than likely have an opinion about what to expect in a "live" concert. The live in person or the "live" on record can be both a good surprise and sadly a bad surprise. For example, take the performance of **Losing Hand** on the studio recording **Keep on Moving by The Paul Butterfield Blues Band.** This composition as well as all the rest of the compositions on this album are way too short. This is especially true of a composition called **Love March.** (This author has heard better versions of this composition-however these recordings seem to be a little muddy)

Okay back to **Loosing Hand**. It's okay on the record-but okay is not good enough for this writer. This author demands to be amazed when listening to music. This author was amazed when he heard **The Paul Butterfield Blues Band perform Losing Hand** live at John's Hopkin's University. The reason it was amazing was the Baritone Saxophone, **Trevor Lawrence.** To this listener's ears, this was just perfect. Then you couldn't imagine just how much your reporter was when part two of a "live" recording had **Loosing Hand** on the list of compositions. When your reporter took this disk home he went right to this composition. It was better than the studio recording as far as giving the musicians time to stretch out. However, there was no Baritone Saxophone solo by **Trevor**

Lawrence. To say the least this your author liked this version of **Losing Hand** but seriously regrated that there was no stellar solo from **Trevor Lawrence,**

With this in mind, your author was quite pleased to see a "live" recording by **John Coltrane** and the quartet he was leading had a whole side of an LP devoted to a "live" recording of **MFT.** Before we turn to reviewing this exciting abet somewhat flawed performance this writer feels it would behoove all of his friends and relatives to know why yours truly puts live as "live" in quotes. As far as this author knows all in-person concerts are recorded in mono. Then they are doctored up in "the studio" to give the stereo effects. So that is why yours truly puts "live" in quotes.

As stated earlier this effort had a whole side of an LP devoted to **MFT.** Now, this had to be a phenomenal feeling of support for **John Coltrane by Impulse! Records** However this was not the first time **Impulse! Records** had done this. The recordings done by **John Coltrane at the Village Vanguard as well as Assentation, Meditations, Kulu Se Mamma, and the "live recordings" in Japan and Seattle** bear whiteness to the fact that the folks at **Impulse! Records** gave their recording artists a whole lot of creative freedom. For example, take **Portrait of Robert Thompson as a Young Man by Archie Shepp** this side long cut that features samplings from **Duke Ellington and what was called "Dixie Land" music as well as the inclusion of a John Phillip Souza march to end this composition, then yours truly does not know what giving the performer total artistic freedom is.** (Note **Charles Ives** preceded **Archie Shepp in this effort when he wrote his second sympathy with Columbia the Gem of The Ocean. ~)**

However, we are not here -or rather you are not here to talk about **Charles Ives.** We are here to talk about this **"Live " recording by The John Coltrane of MFT.**

To begin this version of **The John Coltrane Quartet** has two important changes in this recording. On the first recording of **MFT, the accompanying musicians/composers were**

1) **John Coltrane on Tenor Saxophone and Soprano Saxophones**

2) **Mc Coy Tyner on piano**

3) **Steve Davis on Contrabass**

4) **Elvin Jones on drums**

On the 1963 "live" recording of **MFT, the new members of this quartet replaced Steve Davis and Elvin Jones were Jimmy Garrison on Bass and Roy Haynes on drums.**

This inclusion of **Jimmy Garrison on contrabass was the last time John Coltrane had to replace someone on contrabass. Until John Coltrane left this earth Jimmy Garrison held down his chair. Throughout all of the recordings of John Coltrane, Jimmy Garrison provided more than "Bass lines". And at times when the horns were blasting this could prove to be a daunting task. On this recording, Elvin Jones was replaced by Roy Haynes.**

The absence of **Elvin Jones on drums is quite self-evident**. Gone are the cymbal crashes and polyrhythms that were the "trade -marks" of **Elvin Jones** Instead we have **Roy Haynes** working out with brushes on the snare drum. The other noticeable change is the piano solo by **McCoy Tyner.** Gone is the idyllic breezy feel of the earlier recording. Instead, the listener is treated to one of those hard-hitting two-fisted piano work of **Mccoy Tyner** Instead **McCoy Tyner** plays one astonishing up-tempo solos that just builds and builds to a "perfect wave" and then makes way for **John Coltrane.** After a brief snatch from the original **MFT John Coltrane** carries off this composition in the usual stellar performance he has been known for. And in this writer's opinion, this is yet another recording all Jazz lovers should have. You should have it for at least two reasons. 1) This is proof that **John Coltrane could work with any musician/composer and make amazing music.** 2) **This recording proves how important it is that the live recordings of musicians be supported.**

On another note, this is yet another to support venues that have live music no matter what the type. It is of the utmost importance that live music be supported. Otherwise, the day will come when all the live music venues will be replaced by "DJs' who will only play "music" only fit to get drunk by.

- **John Coltrane "Live at Newport on the Impulse! Label features**

- **John Coltrane on Soprano and Tenor Saxophones**

- **McCoy Tyner on Contrabass**

- **Roy Haynes on Drums**

PS This writer calls this release "flawed" because he misses **Elvin Jones on Drums.** That's no biggie! Should the day come when this writer might need **Roy Haynes on Drums** to help him do a Jazz and Poetry event -rest assured he will be welcomed with open arms.

B 4

Coltrane "live" at The Village Vanguard Again

What a difference three years can make. If the timid listener longs for pleasant relaxing music-then this recording is not a good choice. However, should the listener desire to listen to some amazing stuff then **John Coltrane's "Live" at the Village Vanguard Again** should be on the listening list. As implied in the title this was a return to this classic venue. Although this recording pales in comparison to the output recorded on the **Complete Village Vanguard Sessions.** This multi-disk effort was recorded when the composer/multi-instrumentalist **Eric Dolphy** made what is called **The Standard John Coltrane** a quintet that was also supplemented by other musicians/composers. This is another stellar **John Coltrane** recording. (Note during this time **John Coltrane** also supplemented this unit with **Wes Montgomery on guitar**. Sadly, this reviewer knows if this ensemble made any recordings.

And so, after a three-year hiatus, **John Coltrane returned to The Village Vanguard**. Before we go on it might behoove the listener to know a bit about **The Village Vanguard.**

In February of 1953, **Max Gordon** opened this venue on **Seventh Avenue in the Greenwich Village section of New York City**. Originally this venue featured folk music-beat poetry and jazz. However, in 1967 **The Village Vanguard** became a Jazz-only venue. Both time and space prohibit this writer to go on in length about the list of "who's who" in all forms of Jazz that performed there. However, the curious reader can go to your favorite search or online encyclopedia, or local library to find out more.

The most endearing thing about **The Village Vanguard** was the size of the place. When this writer visited this venue it was as though he was transported into the reconverted basement of a Jazz lover or a reconverted backyard deck. Yes, this place was this small. however, it was the intimacy and the close proximity to the stage that gave this place its ambiance. The other thing that was special about **The Village Vanguard was the owner Max Gordon** who as legend would have it he treated all performers with the utmost respect. And that dear readers are the reasons that all the performers who also made gigs in larger venues chose to perform at **The Village Vanguard.**

This recording was made in 1966 during the last period in the life of **John Coltrane.** It is also the only recording made by this augmented quintet. As the song goes "some changes made" were quite obvious. Gone was **McCoy Tyner who was replaced by Alice Coltrane. Elvin Jones had also left this ensemble and was replaced by Rashid Ali.** (Rumor has it that **Elvin Jones** left this group because he got migraine headaches working with this group.)

John Coltrane's " live" at the Village Vanguard has only three tracks on it. They are **Naima by John Coltrane, The introduction to MFT by Jimmy Garrison, and My Favorite Things.** This is yet another compact disk that this writer is glad this recording has made a compact disk or can be purchased on some downloading venue. Why? Well for starters the **Introduction To My Favorite Thing by Jimmy Garrison** ends side one.

this means the record needed to be turned over. However, as with many recordings that had to be turned over there was always a brief recap of the last song or as in **Ascension** it just reprised the last notes of side a. When this writer heard that **John Coltrane Live At the Village Vanguard** was on the disk, he made a b-line to the nearest store to buy this recording.

In this, the final review of the evolution of **MFT** your poet friend will once again show you why "Jazz is the music of surprise" as Whitney Balliett has told us.

This recording begins with an intriguing contrabass/pizzicato solo. From the onset, the listener wonders just how **Jimmy Garrison** can segue into **MFT.** Since your reporter does not want to spoil this sound of surprise -he will not tell you just how **Jimmy Garrison** managed to segue flawlessly into **MFT.** You dear reader must unlock this magic box to find out about it.

Shortly after **Jimmy Garrison** ends his introduction **John Coltrane** begins with a few musical noodling's that he sets up for his melody statement. It is not as fast as his Newport recording it comes on at a medium tempo. But the listener take note. Just as soon as **Pharoah Sanders** enters this becomes a head-dizzying collage of music. The music swirls and spins like a dervish dancer. To do a play-by-play review would mean that this author would have to write for eons. Suffice it to say that this two-horn ensemble sounds much larger. One reason is the soloists switch instruments when the muse tells them to do so. That means **John Coltrane can be heard on Bass Clarinet and Flute along with his "regular horns" It also means Pharoah Sanders can be heard on flute.** (Note up until the release of this recording your reviewer had a take it or leave it the opinion of **Pharoah Sanders.** However, when your poet friend heard this recording and saw **Pharoah Sanders perform at The Village East** he grasped fully understood what **Pharoah Sanders** was all about. Then later when your reporter was listening to a composition that alternated effortlessly between free jazz and some lovely **Junior Walker** soulful sounds did he get more than a clue about the musical visions of **Pharoah Sanders** This composition is called **Medley Aun, Venus and Capricorn Rising is on his album Tahuid on the Impulse! Label is where you may find this medley.)**

Although the recording might be thirty minutes tops-it seems to go on for a wonderfully long time. Horns come in-horns go-and then with the closing theme we hear **Pharoah Sanders** doing some butterfly-sounding trills to close this set-out. And that is why your reporter knows **John Coltrane "Live" at the Village Vanguard is another favorite on his go-to listening list**

The musicians/composers on this album are.

- **John Coltrane on Tenor and Soprano Saxophones as well as Bass Clarinet and Flute**

- **Pharoah Sanders on Tenor Saxophone and Flute**

- **Allice Coltrane on Piano**

- **Jimmy Garrison on Contrabass/ And Emanuel Rahim on percussion. This recording is on Impulse! Record**

The Village Vanguard jazz club in New York City, 2018

CHAPTER ELEVEN

Photographic Interlude

PEOPLE IN THOUGHT

A Photo Essay

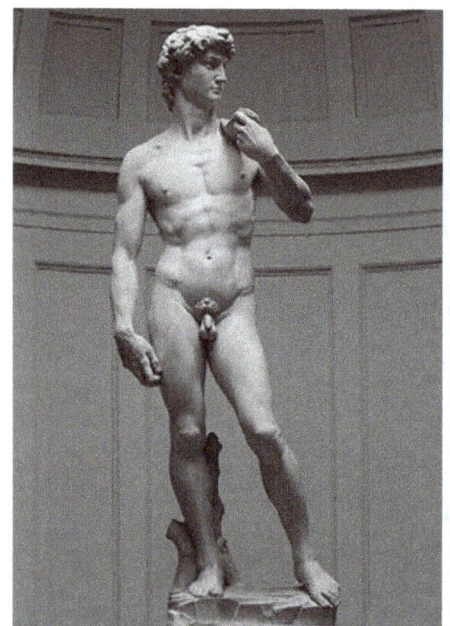

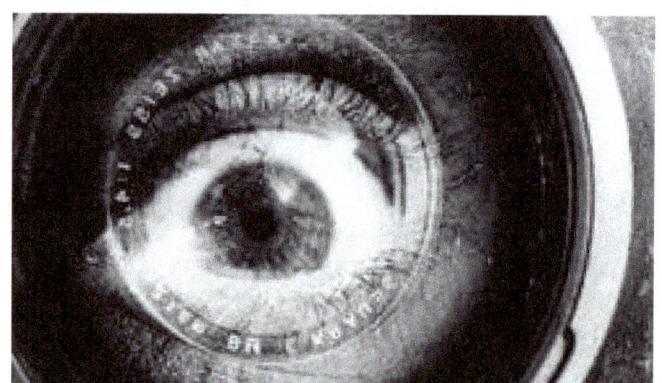

1928) — The Movie Database (TMDB ...

themoviedb.org

Tom Oelschlaeger

I love music.
I cannot listen to music while I do other stuff. My mind always turns to the music and ignores everything else.

Herbie Hancock End Piece

Why is jazz not part of the pop scene anymore?

Herbie Hancock: "Because it's not the music that matters anymore. People don't care about the music itself anymore, but about who makes the music. The public is more interested in celebrities and how a certain artist is more famous than music. It changed the way the audience relates to music. He no longer has a transcendental connection to music and its quality. Just wants the glamour. Jazz doesn't want to be part of it. Do you know why? It's not about humility, or arrogance, a posture "we don't want to be famous, we're underground". None of that. Jazz is about the human soul, not about the appearance. Jazz has values, teaches to live the moment, work together, and especially to respect the next. When musicians gather to play together, you have to respect and understand what the other does. Jazz in particular is an international language that represents freedom, because of its roots in slavery. Jazz makes people feel good about themselves."

Frank Zappa End Piece

"I write the music I like. If other people like it too, fine, they can go buy the albums. And if they don't like it there's always Michael Jackson for them to listen to."

~ Frank Zappa

"Music should be holy. When it becomes a business and the music is designed to make money, then the music changes"

Jerry Garcia

"Do not worry about what your friends think of my music. They listen with their memories only"

Edgar Varese in a letter to this author

Frank Zappa in Paris, early 1970s

Edgar Varese

CHAPTER TWELVE

Section C

What Is Improvision In Jazz (and Blues) And Why Parvenues , Neophytes And People With Little Talent (IF Any) A Limited Should Eschew Trying To Improvise.

By now dear reader you are a little bit familiar with the quote "Jazz is the sound of surprise" that Whiney Ballet spoke. However, in life some surprises are nightmares. You know what this reporter is talking about. If not then let your writer give you some examples. A bad surprise is

1) When you throw a party and that nice guy you know from your job is a mean drunk who must be forcefully ejected from your house

2) You and your wife have been trying to have a baby. Then you find out she is pregnant by another man.

3) While going for a job interview at a Holliday Inn you discover your hubby is having an affair with your mom

4) You are attending what is supposed to be a concert of Avant Guarde African American Classical Music the performers are all white and the music stinks

While this author has absolutely nothing to say about points 1 through 3, he will refer you to the quote by **Jazz Composer and piano performer George Russel** who opined in what was called **The October Jazz Revolution** that "The Avant Guarde is the last refuge for the untalented." And sadly, this is true. Now let us turn our attention to point 4. This example of a "bad surprise" could not be more true when it comes to the untalented. Here's example number one. The renowned **Contrabass performer/ pianist/ composer Charles Mingus** booked a gig for some aspiring musicians to show case their talents. He had these musicians perform behind a curtain. When the performance was over the curtains parted and the audience gave these young musicians a standing ovation. However, the audience was not able to clap long. The "leader" of this ensemble told the audience to stop clapping/ He went on to say that none of these young folk on stage could read music-much less play their instruments. This youth well-wise before his age told the audience they did not need hollow applause . He said instead that what they needed was music lessons that would not only teach them how to perform on their instruments but how to understand music theory. That in a nutshell proves that **George Russel** was right on time.

Another example is **The High Zero Festival held in Baltimore**/ Aside from a few serious composers or sound thinkers like **Neil Feather or tENTATIVELY a cONVIENCE** the rest of these so-called "Avant Guarde" musicians were both fooling themselves and their audience. Aside from the fact these musicians might be performing on things that were not intended to produce music what came out was faux new thing music. This is what happens when truly imaginative composers like Harry Partch or Lamont Young debut their new music and some yokel with a Sears -Robock Tenor Saxophone gets it into his fool head that he could be just like them. It gets even worse when some know-it-all hack musician goes to a performance by either **Neil Feather or tENTATIVELY a cONVIENCE.** They write off what they can't comprehend. That is because these know -it-alls do not know that both these composers/inventors/musicians actually put some serious time crafting their art. **tENTATIVELY a cONVIENCE** has gone so far as to call himself a **"sound thinker" and the results of his efforts "Bood Usic"**

At one time your reporter went to a concert that was billed as a concert of new music. Your reporter remembers seeing some musicians perform **All Set by Milton Babbit and what John Cage called "Cartridge Music "being performed by Karlheinz Stockhausen, David Tutor and John Cage himself**. Your reporter remembers being t-totally enthralled by these presentations. Your reporter knows the difference between T-bone steak and steakums. Sadly, what is offered up at **The High Zero**

Festival held in Baltimore. And on a more personnel note, your author was a member of a ragtag group of musicians and performers with the highbrow intentions and along with yours truly not much musical talent. Heck even the name of the unit **Watermark** smacked of parvenueism. The performance we did were awful and your reporter was embarrassed to be performing on stage with these folks. This is why your reporter will only engage in tape manipulations and then *only at home alone* ! After listing to the greats, the efforts of this group were lackluster at best. That doesn't mean that yours truly does not consider the other participants to be yokels . You could search the globe and never find finer more intelligent and talented folks who were not musicians. However, in spite of the great writing talent and singing ability all but one of this ensemble was a serious musician. She played the conga drums and was a musician/composer that was in quite demand among musician/composers all over Charm City (That's Baltimore to you friend)

Section 2

More On Improvising

Or

"Give The Drummer Some"

Author Unknown

If this weren't enough of a problem for the neophyte improviser-let's toss in another skill this wannabe Jazz (or Blues) improviser. Once again it involves the beat or tempo of the music. In a typical Blues(or any Blues or Blues Related such as Funk or Soul or Reggie) band the drummer is faced with two tasks. The obvious task is keeping a steady beat. The other task/demand is to make the music swing. Obviously playing a straight 4/4 rhythm is not going to cut it, *especially* if the goal of this ensemble is to empower the audience to "get up" and either/or "shake their tail feathers or get up/or down and" boogie". Or as the **Sly And The Family Stone song Dance To The Music** says: "All we need is a drummer/for people only need a beat" However **Duke Ellington** might add this caveat " It don't mean a thing if it ain't got *that* swing"

And getting "that swing" for Blues and Jazz Drummers means "being in the pocket" or providing just the right amount of drumming elan do what must be done. There are several ways the drummer can do this. There is what is called "the backbeat" which is where the accents of this drumming style are on the second and fourth beat. Then there's playing on the beat, in front, and behind the beat. Playing on the beat should be patently obvious to anyone-even those of you who are from Cape Gerardo. Playing before the beat means the drummer anticipates the beat and hits the cymbal just a nano-moment before the beat should be played. Playing behind the beat is just the opposite. Then as if this wasn't enough some drummers perform what are called polyrhythms. This could be not keeping a "straight time" and just keeping time. Polyrhythmic drumming means now the drummer is free to embellish what the other members are performing while the contrabass or bass guitar keeps the beat. At this point, your reporter suggests you listen to **any recording on the Impulse! Label featuring John Coltrane and Elvin Jones or any Art Blakey recording. Other recordings that showcase this approach are Drum Orgy, Drums Around The World and Drums Around The World as well as recordings by the M'boom Percussion Ensemble under the tutelage of Max roach.**

As if this weren't the only thing the drummer-(and all band members) must do there is one other problem. Not all music is performed in the 4/4 beat. Some western music is played in 3/4 time. This is called waltz music. There are three notes to a bar and the quarter note gets the one beat. Then there are other beats. There are 6/8 a faster 3/4 beat and the famous 5/4 beat that the African American Classical Music musician and composer **Max Roach taught the white alto saxophonist Paul Desmond** which became Take Five and really made playing odd time signatures something other Jazz musicians/composers incorporated into their music. Sadly, it was both **Paul Desmond and Dave Brubeck who got all the props for this while Max Roach got none. And it was Max Roach who first started using this time signature.** To quote **Brian Wilson of the Beach**

Boys John Christian "And if that ain't enough to make you flip your lid there's one more thing"[18] A lot of musicians in the sixties began to look to the music of India. Here is one example. One of the compositions recorded at **The Village Vanguard was India by the composer/multi-instrumentalist by John Coltrane is recorded using Indian rhythms or perhaps polyrhythms.** Then there was **Don Ellis** who went to India to study music. After that, he produced an album called **Don Ellis live in 3 2/3/4 time.** This boggles this writer so much that he feels inadequate to even bluff you the reader about what this is. So don't be lazy-go on out and get this album. (along with the other recordings mentioned here)

With all these options facing the serious drummer/percussionist, it is amazing to think that these musicians get dissed the way they do. For example, there is the "joke" that goes like this. What do you call a guy who hangs out with musicians? You call him the drummer. Sadly, rock stars like **Sandy Nelson and Ron Wilson of The Safaris who recorded Wipe Out do not do a thing to debunk this myth.**

---

18 From the song Little Duce Coop

Section 2

The Face Of The Bass/Bass Guitar

Or

"Give The Bass a Taste"

Author Unknown

After looking at the role the of the drummer we now will turn our attention to the contrabass (AKA Double Bass or just Bass) and the Bass Guitar. Lord knows just where the need for a "bass line" or bass accompaniment came from. This writer thinks it harkens back to early **Indian Classical Music** or even earlier to the **Aboriginals of Australia** with the long tubular wind instrument the didgeridoo. Being somewhat of a neophyte in music history your author will leave this point to the real music historians who are free to email this author at <u>magoo1917@earthlink.net</u> to set the record straight. With this in mind let us proceed on. Both the **Indian Classical Music and Aboriginal Classical Music** require the presence of a drone or pedal point instrument. In **Indian Classical Music,** it is the tambura. According to a source on google:" The tambura an **India Stringed Instrument** is a plucked drone instrument used **to accompany instrumental or vocal performances**. The four strings are played open rather than being depressed to alter the note." Listing to the music of sitar performers **Ravi Shanker or Ali Akbar** one can hear a constant drone in the background. That is the sound of a tamboura. This instrument produces what people with much more musical knowledge call a pedal point, in music which is "**A tone sustained through several changes of harmony that may be consonant or dissonant with it**; in instrumental music, it is typically in the bass." Google.

As we move our attention to **Mexican Classical Music** we find an instrument called The **guitarrón Mexicanos**. Once again after going to Google this author found out that "The **guitarrón Mexicanos** (the Spanish name of a "big Mexican guitar", the suffix -on being a Spanish augmentative) or Mexican guitarrón is a very large, deep-bodied Mexican six-string acoustic bass played traditionally in Mariachi groups. Should this writer receive a little help from the muses or anyone out there with more knowledge on these instruments or this topic or on anything else this author has written feel free to email me.

With that in mind let's go down to New Orleans the birthplace of **A. A. C. M.** (aka "Jazz") Originally it was the Tuba that held down the bass line. That was because earlier examples of **A. A. C. M. of the New Orleans Style** Commonly referred to in what this author feels is the condescending term of "**Dixie Land Music**" that was because these early New Orleans ensembles were brass bands. Logic would have it that an uptight contrabass just would not cut it. (Now pause a minute and think about this. If Brass Ensembles were both self-contained units that mobility was of the utmost importance unless you were atlas or the mighty hulk why would you lug a big old contrabass around with an ensemble whose horns would more than likely drown you out anyway?

Fairly soon **A. A C.M** moved "up the river" and all over the country. Your writer does not know just where this change took place. However, somewhere along the line, the tuba was replaced by the contrabass.[19]. [20]Along with that, the multi-percussion section of the brass ensemble was replaced with the drum kit. At the beginning of the History of **A.A.C.M, the drummer kept time on the bass drum. However, as A.A.C.M developed the role of keeping time was moved up to the cymbals.**

Along with these changes, the role of the Contrabass began to grow. Starting with **the contrabassist Jimmy Blanton and moving forward.** The first act of liberation for the contrabassist was the role of the timekeeper playing a straight pedantic bass line to a more skilled and nuanced bass line. For example, there was the **Walking Bass Line.** If one listens to a straight bass line it would sound like this. One -two-three-four. A **Walking Bass Line** just might sound like this. One a two-three a four one a two-three a four. Then with the advent of either piano-less quartets or the drum less ensembles like **The Nat King Cole Trio or The Trio featuring Composer multi-reed performer Jimmy Giuffrie, Compose Contrabass performer**

---

[19] This remained true until **Gill Evans** and others (perhaps) decided to raise the tuba (and French Horn from the dead od "Dixie Land" and incorporate these instruments into various sized ensembles ushered a new type of **A.A.C.M** called "Cool Jazz" and empowering such tuba performing **A.A.C.M** musicians/composers As **Don Butterfield, Ray Draper and Howard Johnson.** The inclusion of the tuba (and the French horn as well) can be heard in many of the well know ensembles. Here are just a few. **John Coltrane Africa Brass, Miles Davis Sketches of Spain and Birth of the Cool, Tuba Jazz by Ray Draper, Mamma Too Tight By Archie Shepp, and the Charles Mingus Brass Ensemble recording made after this unit had performed at the Monterey Jazz Festival.** At times **Trombonist Wayne** performed and soloed with **The Jazz Crusaders** on double belled euphonium (a relative of the tuba) The recorded work of **Tuba/Baritone Saxophonist Howard Johnson** also was heard with quite a variety of ensembles from Archie Shepp to Carla Bley and as said earlier Charles Mingus. In addition to this Ray Draper has performed and recorded with Taj Mahal the leader of many Jazz Fusion ensembles and blues ensembles. The recording musician called The Real thing is the one that comes to this writers mind is The Real thing. The rock composer and musician John Lennon also has Howard Johnson as part of the ensemble on his recording Walls And Bridges. Along with that Howard Johnson has recorded and performed with his own ensembles such as the Howard Johnson Substructure which features a tuba section The Jazz Rock band Blood Sweat And Tears features a tuba solo by the trombonist/tuba performer/composer Dave Bergeron on the Laura Nero composition And when I die. And lastly John Coltrane led what was called his "classic quartet" on a recording called Africa Brass that featured an ensemble that featured mostly tubas, French Horns, and a euphonium. This effort was recorded on Impulse Records. It was his eighth recording for that label.

[20] Here this author must take another sidetrack to talk about the tuba performer/bassist **Red Callender.** Along with being one of the mentors of Bassist Charles Mingus has recorded with a wide spectrum of musicians and groups. The one that sticks out in the mind of this writer is B Bumble And His Stingers. This ensemble did an amazing boogie -Woogie version The Flight of The Bumble Bee by Nikolai Rimsky Korsakov.

Steve Swallow and pianist Paul Bley led to inspiring ensembles of such diversity **Gerry Mulligan and Ornette Coleman**. In these units, the contrabassist was free to do what is called **counterpoint performing.** There is a longer definition that goes on for a bit. However, the first paragraph of this Wikipedia says this **"counterpoint** is the relationship between two or more <u>musical lines</u> (or voices) which are <u>harmonically</u> interdependent yet independent in <u>rhythm</u> and <u>melodic contour</u>.[1] It has been most commonly identified in the <u>European classical tradition</u>, strongly developing during the <u>Renaissance</u> and in much of the <u>common practice period</u>, especially in the <u>Baroque period</u>. The term originates from the <u>Latin</u> *punctus contra punctum* meaning "point against point", i.e., "note against note". And goes into greater detail than is necessary for this tome.

Not only that but the role of a single contrabassist was expanded to perhaps two bassists. The Recording **Herbie Manne at the Village Gate has the composer of Comin' Home Baby augmenting Ahmed Abdul Malik the regular member of this ensemble. Both Assentation by John Coltrane and Free Jazz by Ornette Coleman feature two double bass performers/composers.**

Now let us turn our attention to the Bass Guitar. In the Blues, the Bass Guitarist supports the unit he or she is in by providing just the right amount of oomph or spice. Once again to quote from **Dance To The Music by Sly And The Family Stone "I'm gonna add some bottom so that the dancers just won't hide"** says it all. Looking north to Detroit the sadly underrated Electric Bassist (or bass guitarist) **James Jamerson was part** of the reason Motown Records had the unique style they had.[21]. With the advent of the **Brattish Invasion** which introduced folks over here to the Beatles and the Rolling Stones, another group **Cream which featured Jack Bruce on Bass** presented what was called **The bumble bee bass line, which has to be heard to understand what it is.**[22]

With this out of the way, we will turn our attention to the role of keyboards in the blues and **A.A.C.M**

---

[21] At this point this author would say it would behoove the reader to watch the film **Standing In The Shadows of Motown**

[22] Note both before and after Jack Bruce was in cream he has performed a number of ensembles. The Tony Williams Lifetime group of led by Drummer/composer erstwhile member of one of the ensembles of Miles Davis, Tony Williams is one example. He is also featured on Recordings by the composer/ multi-instrumentalist ensemble leader Carla Bley

Section 3

The Role of Keyboards in A.A..C.M And The Blues

This section should be a "No Brainer" Keyboards in Both Blues and A.A.C. M ensembles adding both a thicker and larger feel to these units. Keyboards give soloists a harmonic cushion to enhance their soloing such as both **Victor Feldman** did with both **Miles Davis** and **Shelley Manne.** However, when listing to the A.A.C.M **Cecil Taylor** or **Thelonious Monk.** Keyboards can also create marvelous solos such as the solos of **Keith Jarret** on both versions of **Forrest Flower** and **Jimmy Smith** did on his amazing solo on **Got My Mojo Workin'** Keyboard soloists can create magic with what are called **Block Chords** Mister Wikipedia tells us about **Block Chords** in these few words What is a block chord? A block chord is **a type of voicing where each of the notes are close together, within an octave.** The great George Shearing popularized the sound of block chords on piano by doubling the highest note of his voicings an octave below, reinforcing the chord to emphasize his melodies. Sadly Mister W. failed to point **Block Chords** in A.A.C.M were perfected and perhaps introduced by **BLACK** musicians and composers such as **Red Garland, Wynton Kelley, McCoy Tyner, Ramsey Lewis,** and others.

Along with providing **Block Chords,** the ensemble keyboard performer can also play contrapuntal lines along with or in clashes with soloists. The music of **Thelonious** or **Cecil Taylor** will show this.

Then if the pianist has a good left hand such as **Cecil Taylor** or **Art Tatum** the need for a contrabass in the rhythm section is eliminated. This goes double for performers who use **bass pedals on their B3 organs** in Blues or A.A.C.M in A.A.C.M the phenomena of the **Organ Trio-basically a quartet sans a contrabass**. Has been and will be the kind of basic unit of a lot of the performers and composers of a more funky-based A.A.C.M. **Jimmy McGriff** and **Groove Holmes** have long done well by this example of music.

But wait the organ or any other keyboard can give your basic A.A.C.M or Fusion A.A.C.M unit the cutting-edge sound that it is needed. **Larry Young** did this with the **Tony Williams Lifetime Ensemble**. **Jan Hammer** has done this with the **Mahavishnu Orchestra** or with **Elvin Jones**. And who could forget **Sun Ra?** This brand of A.A.C.M is way too complex, to sum up in this tome.

But the ensemble is not the only place a performer can be heard. The various types of A.A.C.M solo piano go back to the bordellos and brothels of New Orleans. (In passing this is why a lot of people think A.A.C.M is not serious music. These people argue that because this music came from houses of ill-repute they do not merit a serious listen. However, your writer has mixed emotions about this statement. It's one thing for people to dance and party at a club. It is another thing altogether for people to talk while a non-dance ensemble is performing. Here's the guiding rule. If you would not talk when a western classical ensemble is giving a concert-you should zip your lip at A.A.C.M concerts)

Getting back to the types of solo A.A.C.M solo keyboard performers they range from

1) Boogie Woogie or Barrell House is a two-fisted rolling type of music

2) Stride piano which has a smoother sound

3) Types your writer can't explain such as the solo piano works of **Keith Jarret or Thelonious Monk**

4) Or ragtime-which is true A.A.C.M. because there is no improvisation at all in it

At this point, yours truly must do a tip of the hat to the alpha and omega of A.A.C.M piano-**Art Tatum. When Art Tatum performed all ten fingers of his hands were in constant motion. Whether doing solo work or in any ensemble, the listener will have to remark the way the young Canadian A.A.C.M pianist did when hearing Art Tatum for the first time. He just listened to a solo Art Tatum recording and asked, "How many guys are there on this record?"** And you dear friend will also ask this question too. Stay tuned for the last section-not all improvising is solo improvising.

CHAPTER THIRTEEN

Section 4

Not all improvising is solo improvising.

The Role of The Riff

And

Just A Tip Of The Hat To Those who Arrange The Music

(It is the sincerest and most honest wish of this writer to make this section as brief as possible. And not include two major sections of this tome. One is called How This Writer Discovered A.A.C.M and the Blues. The other is The Blues And The Jews. A Reflection On The Sympathetic

Chord That Vibrates Between All People Who Wished They Knew How It Would Feel To Be Free (And Celebrate The Freedom Of All Humanity) This will be published in the expanded version of On Silence And Other Non-Sounds. This is another book by this author on Amazon.com)

There are two common misconceptions about improvising.

1) Improvising is just done in the soloing, and just by the soloist. (Sound of Buzzer From The Family Feud Television Show) Wrong! Sometimes when a soloist is playing the introduction or the conclusion of a composition, this soloist (or more soloists) might play some embellishing notes. Sometimes a singer might put an inflection or an emphasis on a certain phrase of the song. This is called "phrasing". (Note this is a skill all good actors have. Public speakers, performance poets, and all who "read out" must learn and use it well). In these instances, these little embellishments are improvised. Therefore, should be called "Improvised Spontaneous Composing" For a few examples check out **Losing Hand by The Paul Butterfield Blues Band "live" on Electra Records, Any Recording of Charlie Parker of Embraceable You. Naima by John Coltrane on John Coltrane "Live at The Village Vanguard Again! On Impulse! Records. How High The Moon on Mack The Knife/Ella In Berlin on Verve Records.**

2) Collative Improvising is always hectic and confusing. (Sound of Buzzer From The Family Feud Television Show) Wrong! Listen to **Any Bill Evans Trio Recording on the Riverside Label. This is collective Improvising. Then Listen to Very Tall by Oscar Peterson and Milt Jackson on Verve Records**

The role of the riff. Sometimes when the music of a Blues or A.A.C.M. ensemble gets to be quite exciting one or more members of the ensemble will play one or two or more (perhaps) sympathetic notes as the soloist is soloing. This is not an attempt to drown out the soloist. On the contrary, it is the desire of these musician (s) to generate more excitement for the soloist. These spirited accompaniments are called "riffs" and can be either spontaneous or arranged. Lastly, there might be a few improvised codas at the end of any Blues or A.A.C.M composition. These might be called riffs or improvised codas.

Now finally we need to tip our hats to the arrangers. From **Billy Strayhorn to Duke Ellington to Carla Bley and Melba Liston and Charles Mingus or Gill Evans**, the role of proper and good arranging and orchestrating can change the very essence of the composition. This act of restructuring the basic framework of a song is sort of akin to remaking a movie. And just like the remake of a movie these arrangements must be created to capture the listeners' attention. (Gee whiz folks this writer just might include a section called The arranger's Touch in that yet-to-be-published expanded version of On Silence And Other Non-Sounds)

And dear readers this is all for now about why this writer finds The Blues and Jazz (African-American Classical Music) so amazing. These music forms actually allow the musician(s) to spontaneously compose in both a concert hall concert, a festival, a more intimate setting, or a get-together with other musicians for some off-the-cuff performing. (This is called a Jam Session. Perhaps this author will wax eloquent on this at another time). This is what Whitney Balliett called

"**The Sounds of Surprise**" and what this reviewer called "**The Sounds of Surprise/pain /joy/hope/agony/ecstasy and any other human emotion!**" This is why you dear reader should do what John Hendricks admonished you to do in his one-word poem "Jazz" and that would be "Listen" **Square Bizz** Alan Barysh

Section 5 The Arrangers Touch

At this point, your author would like to talk briefly about the important role of the arranger in A.A.C.M and other related music(s) such as in traditional Rhythm and Blues-not that tripe that calls itself R@B, horn-driven blues bands, and all those fusion/jazz-rock ensembles and in other musical configurations. In a good working musical unit if the group decides to "cover" or reinterpret another piece of music or if this ensemble or solo artist wants to present this form of music in a different light, then the search for an original sound depends on how this revised presentation is arranged. Let us proceed.

At this point, your writer feels it would behoove you to listen to the following examples of arrangements.

1) **The Happy Go Lucky Local by the Duke Ellington Orchestra**

2) **Night Train by Jimmy Forrest**

3) **Night Train by James Brown**

4) **Night Train by Oliver Nelson from his album recorded in Los Angles**

For purposes of clarity, we shall call these examples C1 through C4 in order of their listing. C1 starts off at a jolly tempo. The wah-wah trumpets give this composition a "bouncy" quality to it. This composition is actually the precursor to all the rest of the examples. It had **Duke Ellington** written all over it that is because both **Duke Ellington and his comrade in** arms the pianist/arranger labored hard in "the vineyards " to create **this sound!** Now we go to the original version C2) This is the one that is associated with strippers and strip clubs. This version is raunchy-funky and well flat-out sexy. In C3 **James Brown** speeds up the tempo and all the funk is un-funked. This is a family-friendly version of **Night Train** By the time we hear the **Oliver Nelson** version this interpretation might very well be background music for a really hip Amtrack television commercial. Not only that but **Oliver Nelson** gives the guitarist **Mel Brown** room to stretch out and really make this composition his own.

In order to make this section more exciting listen to the following examples of musical arrangements.

1) **Any version of The Star-Spangled Banner**

2) **The Star-Spangled Banner By Jimi Hendrix**

3) **The Star-Spangled Banner by The Carla Bley Orchestra**

4) **Zippa -De Doodah from the Song of The South**

5) **Zippa-De Doodah by The Sun Ra Archestra**

6) **All of the Impulse! Recording Out of the Hot by Gill Evans**

7) **The original Porgy and Bess Cast Recording**

8) **Porgy and Bess by Miles Davis and Gill Evans**

9) **Down By the Riverside by Elvis Presley**

10) **Down by the Riverside by Mahalia Jackson**

11) **Down by the Riverside by the Oliver Nelson Big Band in Los Angles on Impulse! Records**

12) Any version of You Are My Sunshine

13) You Are My Sunshine by George Russel on The Outer View featuring Shelia Jordan singing the song

14) My Favorite Things from the original cast recording

15) All John Coltrane's versions of My Favorite Things

At this point, your author does not want to belabor the point. Better the music should speak for itself. However, this author implores you to listen and do nothing but listen. No, do not do house cleaning. No, do not pay bills with these examples as background music. Do not listen to these examples in your car while you are at the wheel! Listen to these compositions at home in whatever chair makes you feel comfy. Listen with a refreshing drink-some snack or whatever will put you "in the mood" If you must listen while traveling listen with headphones on. Listen to the music! Why? Because music was created not only to be performed but to be listened to without any distractions that have you keeping your clothes on. Music should be at the forefront of your listening experience. The problem of this modern world is people who listen to music and daydream or as the **Rock Group Stephanwolf said:" Let the sound take you away"** Yes let go listen -listen to the music-listen to how the instruments and vocalists blend into one another or clash against each other. Listen to how the ensemble backs up or clashes with the soloist. Listen to how the soloist(s) with the aid of the other musicians breathe new life into these arrangements. Yes, let the music teach you that there is nothing wrong with" doing nothing" but listening. Should some non-listening -no real thinking yokel with the attention span of Jim Morrison in the can criticize you ask him this question. If spending whole days watching your favorite TV series is not wasting time then broadly widening your musical horizons is just fine and dandy. And if they do not like it-TOUGH TOENAILS!

CHAPTER FOURTEEN

Part Three

Hidden In Plain Sight

The Black Codes

And Gospel Music

"Hidden in plain sight" is an old "folk saying". To many, this phrase might be an oxymoron. However, if one were to think about the art of camouflage, the phrase makes perfect sense. In Gospel music, this phrase will surely ring true. However, before going into what little this author knows about what was called "The Black Codes" let us go back to the time of Aesop's Fables. This author remembers learning that the poet/author Aesop told stories that were supposed to be fiction. However, these allegedly simple folk tales were very astute commentaries by Aesop about the politics of his time. Aesop wrote these fables in a way that he could communicate with the people he thought needed to know what was going on *without* letting those he wished to be kept "in the dark"-in the dark.

Now let us fast forward to the antebellum south. Even though the old slaver had his overseers and house slaves working for him, he still distrusted his slaves. That is why when the "diver man" who was the old slaver's eyes and ears saw his master was out riding around and the slaves were silently working he would holler out something like "make a sound" and the slaves would start to sing.

However, what the overseer and the slave master did not know was the hidden meaning in these seemingly innocuous Gospel Songs. For example, the first slave ship to arrive in this country was the Good Ship Jesus. So, when the slaver heard the slaves singing "Steel away to Jesus" he *thought* the slaves were talking about dying and going up to heaven. This made the old slaver happy. What he did not know was the slaves were singing about escaping from his plantation. When the slaves sang "Follow the Drinking Gourd" the slaver had no idea that the slaves were giving instructions about where to go after they left the plantation. These are a few examples of the Black Code. Another example is this. In all Gospel songs, the references to "The River Jordan" were actually references to the Mississippi River. This river separated some of the states that were slave states from the northern non-slaving states. So, when the slaves sang

"Jordon River is deep and cold

Chills the body -but not the soul

Keep your eyes on the prize

Hold on"

Or

Deep river, my home is over Jordan.

Deep river, Lord, I want to cross over into campground.

Oh, don't you want to go to that gospel feast?

That promised land, where all is peace?

Not only that-but these slaves would use the "make a noise" rule to serve their own purposes. It worked like this. First, the slaver forbade the slaves to play any form of drum. That is because the slaver feared the slaves were using "the talking drum" to communicate with one another. However, the slaver did not prohibit his slaves from going to church.

With this in mind, the slaves would go to church and under the guise of having a church service would plot how they were going to escape from the plantation. Sometimes the preacher would preach a sermon using the bible as a "book code"[23] This form of communication was used by **Nat**

---

[23] For more information on Book Codes this author recommends you see the **Alec Guinness movie Our Man In Havana.**

Turner as he organized his slave rebellion. [24][25] With that in mind, the slaves often met to plot and plan in secret. In order to keep from having the real deal about what they were up to the slaves would have a look out or look out's perched in a tree looking out to see if any snoopers were snooping around the church. If they were the lookout would sing

(Way down yonder by myself)
(And I couldn't hear nobody pray)

Oh Lord, I couldn't hear nobody pray
Couldn't hear nobody pray
Oh, way down yonder by myself
And I couldn't hear nobody pray

Oh Lord, I couldn't hear nobody pray
Couldn't hear nobody pray
Oh, way down yonder by myself
And I couldn't hear nobody pray

In the valley
(Couldn't hear nobody pray)
On my knees
(Couldn't hear nobody pray)
With my burden

---

[24] The use of the Bible based book code used in the movie **Matewan.** Without ruining the plot-suffice it to say a young preacher uses this Bible Based Book quote to achieve a positive response to something slanderous

[25] For another more humorous example of the Black Codes read **Tambourines To Glory by Langston Hughes**

(Couldn't hear nobody pray)

And my Savior

(Couldn't hear nobody pray)

Oh Lord, I couldn't hear nobody pray

Couldn't hear nobody pray

Oh, way down yonder by myself

And I couldn't hear nobody pray

Chilly water

(Couldn't hear nobody pray)

In the Jordan

(Couldn't hear nobody pray)

Crossin' over

(Couldn't hear nobody pray)

Into Canaan

(Couldn't hear nobody pray)

Oh Lord, I couldn't hear nobody pray

I couldn't hear nobody pray

Oh, way down yonder by myself

And I couldn't hear nobody pray

Hallelujah

(Couldn't hear nobody pray)

Troubles over

(Couldn't hear nobody pray)

In the Kingdom
(Couldn't hear nobody pray)
With my Jesus
(Couldn't hear nobody pray)

Oh Lord, I couldn't hear nobody pray
I couldn't hear nobody pray
Oh, way down yonder by myself
And I couldn't hear (No, Lord, I couldn't hear)
I couldn't hear (No, Lord, I couldn't hear, Lord)
And I couldn't hear nobody pray
(Couldn't hear nobody pray, nobody)[26]

When the church-going slaves heard this-they knew trouble was afoot-and they had best be singing to keep the busy bodies busy doing something else. These slavers were clueless as to just what the slaves were singing about. With that in mind, can you figure out what the lyrics of this song were *actually* about?

1 Hush, Hush, Somebody's callin' my name.
Hush, Hush, Somebody's callin' my name.
Oh, Hush, Hush, Somebody's callin' my name.
O my Lord, O my Lord, what shall I do?
What shall I do?

---

[26] (Transcribed from the Patti Page recording by Mel Piddle - Jan 2011)

2 Sounds like Jesus. Somebody's callin' my name.

Sounds like Jesus. Somebody's callin' my name.

Oh, Sounds like Jesus. Somebody's callin' my name.

O my Lord, O my Lord, what shall I do?

What shall I do?

3 Soon one morning, death come creepin' in my room.

Soon one morning, death come creepin' in my room.

Oh, Soon one morning, death come creepin' in my room.

O my Lord, O my Lord, what shall I do?

What shall I do?

4 I'm so glad, got me religion on time.

I'm so glad, got me religion on time.

Oh, I'm so glad, got me religion on time.

O my Lord, O my Lord, what shall I do?

What shall I do?

5 I'm so glad trouble don't last always.

I'm so glad trouble don't last always.

Oh, I'm so glad trouble don't last always.

O my Lord, O my Lord, what shall I do?

What shall I do?

With this in mind, let us look at another aspect of Gospel music and the rebellious nature of it. This author finds that Gospel music has an edgy feel to it. As the composer/instrumentalist **Cannonball Adderley** said in the introduction to the **Bobby Timmons** composition **This Here** the song was "Simultaneously a shout and a chant. Providing you know anything about church music. That is soul church music. I don't mean no Bach Chorales-Church music"[27]

So, it is with Gospel music. This is and was a celebration of Black/African consciousness and pride. This is music that truly is a joyful noise. Gospel music was a way for the slaves to assert their humanity. Gospel music has also had a profound effect on the civil rights movement. With only a few minor changes the song **Woke Up This Morning With My Mind on Jesus became Woke Up This Morning With My Mind On Freedom or**

Ain't Gonna Let Nobody Turn Me 'Round (lyrics)

Ain't gonna let nobody turn me 'round,
turn me 'round, turn me 'round,
Ain't gonna let nobody turn me 'round
I'm gonna keep on a-walkin', keep on a-talkin', Marching up to freedom land.

Ain't gonna let Nervous Nelly turn me 'round, turn me 'round,
Ain't gonna let Nervous Nelly turn me 'round, I'm gonna keep on a-walkin', keep on a-talkin', Marching up to freedom land.

---

[27] **Cannonball Adderley-Live In San Francisco-Riverside Records**

Ain't gonna let Chief Pritchett turn me 'round, turn me 'round,
Ain't gonna let Chief Pritchett turn me 'round, I'm gonna keep on a-walkin', keep on a-talkin', Marching up to freedom land.

Ain't gonna let Mayor Kelly turn me 'round, turn me 'round,
Ain't gonna let Mayor Kelly turn me 'round, I'm gonna keep on a-walkin', keep on a-talkin', Marching up to freedom land.

Ain't gonna let segregation turn me 'round, turn me 'round,
Ain't gonna let segregation turn me 'round,
I'm gonna keep on a-walkin', keep on a-talkin', Marching up to freedom land.

Just kept the same lyrics.

Some will say the chord changes to Gospel Music are the same as the chord changes to the music known as the Blues. This author will not comment on this. It would be better left to those who are more knowledgeable. Suffice it to say this edginess to Gospel music has had a profound influence on Jazz as well. Listen to **Ray Charles sing I've Got A Woman.** Then listen to the **Atlantic Records album Blues and Roots by Charles Mingus.** After that listen to both versions of **Better Get It (Hit) In Your Soul by Charles Mingus. The first version is on the Columbia Record album Mingus Ah Um The Second Version is on the Impulse! Recording Mingus-Mingus-Mingus-Mingus**. You will be amazed by both. However, the brief coda performed by the **Composer/Tenor saxophonist Booker Ervin** will amaze you. Starting with the Gospel-inspired stride piano introduction by the **multi-instrumentalist/composer Jaki Byard** and leading into the mini-tenor saxophone solo by **Booker Ervin** this illustrates the inherent influence of Gospel music in the world today. This influence can be heard in the inclusion of **Going Home in the New World Symphony by Antonin Dvorak**.

Looking back on history this author ponders this question. What if the slavers saw the real threat to the institution of slavery as those who "tamed the west" saw in the **Ghost Dance** that some of the indigenous people of the west performed? Fortunately for the history of music, the slavers were too stupid to see this threat. Sadly, the pioneers and the settlers who "tamed the west" saw the **Ghost Dance** as a threat to their existence. They felt the Ghost Dance empowered these people -and therefore outlawed this practice. However, history has a beautiful way of doing things.

During the Second World War when the North American Troops needed a way to send encoded messages back and forth it was the **Navajo tribe that used their native language to transmit messages back and forth between the various section of the US Army.** Thus, confusing the Nazis who with all the bruhaha they ululated about what was going on had no more knowledge about this "Than a crab's eye on the end of a stick"[2829]

Poetic Coda

"Shout Sister Shout

Shout brother Shout"

"Can the church day AMEN!"

---

[28] **William S. Burroughs Naked Lunch page 131**
[29] For more on this subject see the movie **Wind Talkers**

The Big Book About Sounds

And

Once again

Everything's okay

Like Duke Ellington said it would be

Come Sunday

From the preacher's pulpit

To the choir section

To the amen corner of James Baldwin

The sounds of

What Langston Hughes called

"Tambourines To Glory" can be heard in church

The gospel sanctified church.

Sing hallelujah

This rough edged

Music ripped from the suffering of

Slaves

And former slaves

Shows just how things of power

Things of great beauty

Can be created by those with nothing to loose

This is powerful praise music

This is soul-stirring music

Ain't no other prayerful music composed by composers from Europe can make God up in Heaven Shake a leg

Or make the angles sing along

This is a music of

Self-/human pride

While this music spoke volumes to those who were homeless in the

"Great American Democracy Experiment"

It fell on deaf ears as the slavers and their families said

"My how those colored folks can surely sing in that childish way of theirs"

Yeah right!

Part Two

Sing Hallaugha

Sing Halaugha

Sing Halaugha

Sing Hallaugha

From the amen corner

And unto the universe

Sing Hallaugha

Sing Hallaugha

Shake your tambourines of glory

And your tail feathers too

Lift every voice and sing

Sing Hallaugha

Though the water is cold

Wade in the water

Keep your eyes on the prize

Hold on

For

We are soldiers in the army

We got to fight

Until we have to die

We got to hold up the blood-stained banner

we got to hold it up

until we die

sing Hallaugha

for we are climbing Jacob's ladder

Sing Hallaugha

And come and go with me to that land we are bound

And

Ain't no stopping us NOW!

End Piece

But What Happened To The Music?

(A Poetic End Piece)

"You've taken my blues and you've gone

You mix 'em up on Broadway and fix 'em up in operas

So they don't sound like me, yup

You done taken my blues and gone

But someday, someone's gonna stand up for me

And sing about me and write about me, Black and beautiful

It'll be me, I reckon, yep, it'll be me"

Langston Hughes, Harlem Renaissance, for the blues people

What happened to the music?

We sixties rebels wonder that all the time!

What happened to the music?

Videos killed some of it!

Disco killed some of it!

Misogamy killed some of it!

Love of money killed some of it!

History revisionism killed some of it!

(Example Black youth for the most part know who Michael Jackson is

They do not know

Milt Jackson

Let alone George and Jonathan)

Langston Hughes said

"You've taking mu blues and gone!"

Now he could bemoan the fact that

The same you

Has

Taken his Jazz and gone

Taken his African American Classical music and gone

Taken his hip-hop/rap and gone

(Gone is revolutionary-minded rap

Here is a

Misogyny filled "music"

Chills the soul

Gone is the urgency of rap

Vulgarized Videos of

Afro-Centric Roman Orgies replete with women sex-objecting themselves

And sadly, liking it

"Money doesn't talk it swears"-Bob Dylan

You've taken the Jazz Clubs and gone

The clubs have been clubbed out of existence

By

DJ'S

Who spin tired old music to the delight of a club owners bottom line

You've taken our Jazz Festivals and morphed them into something that barely resembles Jazz Festivals!

Do you think they would do that to
Bach Festivals?
So once again your poet asks
Where has all the music gone?
And more importantly
Where do we go to get it back?-

CHAPTER FIFTEEN

End Piece 2

By

Arthur Blakey II

I had a great admiration for my great-uncle Mosley, who was a great country-blues guitarist and could blow a mean harp.

I once asked him could you teach me the blues, and he told me, "I can't do it". I asked why, and he said, "Well son, the blues is not something you can teach. Now I can show you some chords or I can teach you scales and such, but kid, the blues is something that is inside you, and if you look deep enough, you will feel it inside you too. Everybody's got the blues in their heart. All we bluesmen do is grab a hold of it and bring it to life."

So, then he challenged me to see if I had an angle on what the blues is all about.

At first, I said, "It's music." Big-uncle Mosley just laughed at me.

Second, I said it is "Technique". He grunted.

Now I had all the respect in the world for my great-uncle, but I began to think that all this nonsense of "screaming from the soul" and "the sorrow of the heart" was all just the ramblings of a crazy-old man, until months later, he died in his sleep. It was said that he died peacefully, but I was truly saddened by his death that I couldn't stop crying.

I thought of his words, "the sorrow in your heart, the screaming of your soul". I never felt such pain and sorrow before his passing.

A few days after his funeral, still grieving and still crying, my mother came to console me. She told me that his last wish was for me to have his most prized guitar, and that someday maybe you will know what the blues is all about.

Then I felt me sadness melt to bittersweet joy when I held his old guitar in my hand and strummed out a slow blues progression in E minor, just as he had taught me, and then I told my mother, "I think I am learning now!"

{P.S. My great-uncle was my first guitar teacher when I was nine years old, and I although there are many others respectfully, I have learned and grew from, but no other has taught me the life lesson of soul-searching like he did. I was thirteen when he passed away. Big-uncle Mosley, your spirit lives on in me...RIP!} -Crazy Art

End Piece Three

Excerpt From Coming of Age In New Milford
By This Author

Now let me tell you a word or two about Pastor Barnes. Some Saturday nights, he'd have me drive him to Harlem. There he'd sit in at a place called Small's Paradise. He would knock them dead on that B3. I remember the first time he sat in. He had read in a paper called *The Village Voice* that there were open jam sessions in a bar in Harlem. So, he asked me to drive him down. When we came in the music stopped you could hear a cigarette drop--no you could hear the ashes fall off the cigarette fall. Pastor Barnes walked in cool as a Miles Davis solo and politely asked if he could sit in on the B3 (that's short for Hammond B3 Organ).[30] The musicians on the stand looked at each other and said yes.

He hardly had time to sit down at the keyboard when they launched into a way up-tempo version of "Cherokee," which is a *real* hard standard.

---

[30] For more information about Jam Sessions see another end piece.

And if that weren't enough they would change to a different key every chorus. Well Pastor Barnes hung in there with every key change, and traded fours with the best of them. From start to finish he was on top of his game. He was so good the musician on the stand gave him a hand when the song was over.

Well from then on, he was *always* welcomed. Heck they even let him park his car in their private lot. Just as soon as he stepped in the door, Tiny the bartender would holler, "Rev Barns is in the house! All you half steppers back away from that B3. Let *the man* show you how it's done." By the way Tiny was a 6-foot-tall 250 plus bartender. I think they called him Tiny as a sarcastic name. And Pastor Barnes would make his way up to the bandstand and launch into "Cherokee" or "C Jam Blues" or "Donna Lee" as if this was his *last times* to play in public.

And while he was on stage, Miss Jones, the proprietor's wife, would come out from the kitchen and say, "Mr. Will, you must be hungry driving all that distance from New Milford. I got a nice plate of smothered pork chops; greens and macaroni and cheese just for you. Oh, and here's some hot buttered biscuits and lime Kool Aide. Boss says it's on the house ona count of you driving Pastor Barnes here. You sure you are Jewish? I swear that in all my life I've never seen a Jewish boy tear up them pork chops like you do! Hava another, they're small but save room for that banana pudding." Oh gosh those were some good days.

End Piece Three

Another End Piece From Coming of Age In New Milford By This Author

<u>Almost Grown</u>

"Don't bother us leaves us alone! Anyway, we're almost grown!" –

"Almost Grown"

by Chuck Berry

First a little poem from my past:

A Tribute to Voluntary Exiles from Suburbia. 4/9/98

<u>Introduction</u>

This poem was inspired by two other poems "Howl" by Allen Ginsburg and "A Tribute to Solid Soul" by the Baltimore poet Lassana Bill Harvey. I think you can find that poem in his book *21 Pieces*. Read the whole book at once!

"I Used To Be A White American, but I Gave It up In the Interests of Humanity." -

Slogan on the front of a T-shirt produced
by the Group Refuse & Resist!

This is dedicated to all those people who abandoned their white roles that were given to them at birth to go out into the world to search for the truth, those suburban hostages who grew up Chasin' The Trane, waiting for a chance to make some Giant Steps away from the world of white bread and mayonnaise, the young singers who heard Lady Day's swan songs and discovered a world of melody outside of Mrs. Huckleberry's music class, or found out that ballet wasn't all there was to The Dance slow as they awkwardly caressed their one and only while a Basement Diva on a 45 sang "This is dedicated to the one I love."

All those daring souls who were bored by the Beatles and secretly prayed each night for some hip English doctors give Ringo an urgently needed Art Blakey/Elvin Jones transfusion into his tired European blood.

The Paul Butterfields, Janis Joplins, Mike Bloomfield's, Ginger Bakers, John Mayell's and Eric Clapton's who pointed us in a different direction, where we could discover: Little Walter, Bessie Smith, B.B. King, Elvin Jones, J.B. Lenoir, Robert Johnson and a whole Diaspora of music, all those Dolphyites and Mingusphiles and Rassanists and Monkites who cursed Ian Anderson under their breaths and wished he'd publicly say how much of a debt he owed to Roland Kirk, the way Zappa did for Varese and Stravinsky, the adventurous souls who knew Led Zeppelin was a bunch of hot air, and who could care less about Elton John, these lovers of good music in any form who dug sounds not skins, who waited for the latest Coltrane album as if it were the word from on high, and followed every personnel change in the Jazz Messengers very seriously and knew that *not* knowing about these changes could be spiritually fatal, who were too young to be beatniks and two old for Generation X, who remember where they were when Monk died, and who can't understand why Booker Ervin isn't a household name, the bebop boomers who grew up staying up at night to hear some d.j. in a distant college town play Ornette Coleman in the wee hours of the morning, body hidden under a blanket ear pressed against the speaker of a cheap transistor radio, hoping dad and mom couldn't hear the music, and wishing they had cash enough to move to New York where the Jazz runs hot and cold 24/7, those pastoral youngsters of the petit bourgeoisie who found truth in a song by Smoky and saw the profound words in the music of Little Richard and Louis Jordan, and if given the opportunity, would have joyously traded in the Holy Grail for a couple of mint condition out-of-print virgin vinyl Sarah Vaughn records. (After all it was just a cup.)

All those kids who grew up and kept on listening a discovered that there *is* a link between Fela and 'Trane and James Brown and Betty Carter and Sade, who realized that tradin' fours was more important than tradin' cards and twelve bars of anything done right was more potent than *any drink*, those members of the Church of Saint Fitzgerald, and the Sacred Order Of Saint Mary Lou Williams, whose leaders included Queens, Counts, Dukes and maybe a Baron or two, a pork pie wearing tenor saxophone playing President, and the three most self-effacing Kings there ever were, the stumbling King who was almost forgotten, the King who said he was born under a bad sign, and the most famous King who complained that every day he had the blues, who saw the saxophone as a sacred horn and the trumpet as a vehicle for channeling the truth to a sleeping world that needed a wakeup call as badly as Bird needed to lose his habit.

Hail to the outcasts of the white middle class who came home to Mother Earth with joy in their bodies and hope in their hearts scatting "Confirmation" and "Night In Tunisia" in little child harmonies in the key of B Natural and C Sharp!

End Piece Four

Excerpt from The soon (but not too soon) rewritten and
digitally remastered version of The Madwoman of Federal Hill![31]
As well as some new stuff.

Miles Smiles Upon Me
AND
Buys Me A Drink!
Twice!
First Time

Let's see I do actually believe it was the era when Miles Davis was
fronting a quintet that featured: Wayne Shorter on Saxophones, Herbie
Hancock on Piano, Ron Carter on Bass, and Tony Williams on Drums. It was
in the autumn of some year or other. The leaves were turning colors, and
for the most part, were still on the trees. I remember I was walking in
Central Park on a Sunday afternoon with my then-wife Harriet Silver -
Barysh-soon to be the ex-Harriet Silver-Barysh. We stopped so I could
show her where I met Janis Joplin-who was desperately trying *not* to look
like Janis Joplin. As a matter of fact-had, had she *not* come up to me and
showed me her driver's license I would not have known who she was.

---

[31] Note since this story and the one about Jimmy Giuffrie were written before this author stopped talking about
himself in the second person-it behooved him to keep the integrity of the story and keep the use of the first person
singular. Thanks, A H R B MEOB! Oh, and there won't be any bold type here either!

Yes, it was she who came up to me and sat down on the bench I was sitting on and calmly asked "smoke?". I said "huh?" Then she said: "Don't worry babe. I ain't no nark. I just wanna share a joint with someone who can like talk to me like I was just a regular chick. You see I'm Janis Joplin- and I just finished doing a show at the Filmore East and like I just had to split the scene to like to be with some real folks who weren't gonna fawn all over me-give me some coke and then try and ball me. So, like are cool with getting a little high and not trying to get in my pants?"

Janis Joplin

Joplin in 1970

I nodded and said "Yeah sure just getting high with you will be just fine. Oh, and you can keep the roach" So we got high and talked a little about this and that. She did most of the talking. She talked about even though she was a star-that she felt alone amongst her fans. She waxed eloquently about just getting out and about by herself and just being alone. Then when we finished her joint she reached into her purse and pulled out two sort of cool RC colas and two moon pies. And while we were sipping and munching she said" "You got an old lady"

I replied:" My mom lives up in Connecticut"

Janis Joplin said:" No like a regular chick a girlfriend. You got a regular chick?"

"Yes" was the answer. At the time I was dating a young lady named Sylvia Darling (Square Biz She lived at 106 MacDougal Street.) So, Janis Joplin asked me if she could have her phone number. Without thinking twice, I wrote it down -and gave it to her. [32] Then she said " Let's go over to the Plaza. That's where I'm staying. You can call her from the lobby. I gotta go up and like get my beauty rest before I go out to some fancy ass party on what these cats call The Island."

On the way over to The Plaza Hotel, she said she told me that all she wanted to do was go on a shopping spree with a "regular chick" have lunch and call it a day. We parted ways outside the Plaza Hotel because she did not want some "snoopy ass photographer taking our pictures and putting

---

[32] Those were the days I could remember all the phone numbers I needed to know. I still remember my childhood number. It was EL-gin 5-4350. Still can't remember my Facebook password.

them on the front page of The Daily News with some kind of stupid caption like who is the new mystery man in Janis Joplin's life?"

She went in first and I just went in and called Sylvia Darling who was more than a little bit elated to hear the news. To make a long story short. Janis called-they went shopping. Janis bought Sylvia her latest album and autographed it. Then according to my then girlfriend, Sylvia Darling-they went to a place called Hamburger Heaven and had what Sylvia Darling said was "a nice lunch"

After I told Harriet my then-wife-soon to leave me for a Mexican Prizefighter that story she said: "Say Al I to quote Guess Who I Saw Today? I know a nice little French Café and bar. Let's go there for lunch?" And so, we did.

And as that very same song says, "As my eyes became accustomed to the gloom" the two of us waited at the bar until the Mature De found us a table. While we were awaiting notice from this fellow we ordered a drink from the bar. My then wife-soon to be my ex-wife pointed out that there were a lot of West Point students dressed up in their fancy West Point attire and I reminded her that was probably because the West Point Football Team was in New York for a game. About the same time, I told my dear then-wife this I heard a well-dressed Black man sitting next to us. He was trying to strike up a conversation with this West Pointer and asked him two maybe three times why there were so many West Point Cadets in town. Although I could plainly hear what this man was saying-apparently the cadet couldn't.

Then in my most friendly and still sarcastic voice, I said to the man sitting to me: "Excuse sir I think there's a football game in town between West Point and some other team. You will have to forgive him. He's from West Point-you know a lot of those guys there are hard of hearing. It comes from them shooting off all those cannons during their school year. You know they have to shoot off lots and lots of cannons before they graduate. And sooner or later they get hearing problems. That's why you see so many army officers who wear hearing aids"

This ticked off the cadet who said he was not deaf. So, I asked him if he was not deaf-how come he could hear me when I was further away than the man who was next to him.

When the man next to me heard what I said he turned to me and asked what was soon to be my ex-wife and I were drinking. I told him and he ordered a round of drinks for all of us. Then he introduced himself to us. With an outstretched hand, he said" "I'm Miles Davis" We said pleased to meet you and I told him how blown away I was when I first heard his album with Gill Evans. He thanked me. Then we chit-chatted about him and music. I told him I had most of his albums and I really enjoyed listening to them. And as we were jaw -boneing, this West Pointer was just falling all over himself apologizing and saying how he didn't know he was Miles Davis and he also had all of his albums. Miles Davis turned to him and said the profanity version of "buzz off "left a fifty-dollar bill for the bartender and just walked out the door. Then this Cadet tried to start a conversation with us!

That's when I pulled rank and said: "Like Miles said buzz off" Then the bartender asked if this fellow was bothering us. At the same time, we were told our table was waiting-so off we went to enjoy a real fine French lunch.

Davis in his New York City home, c. 1955–56; photograph by <u>Tom Palumbo</u>

Second Time

Lew Frisch and I had been good friends ever since we went to a summer camp called Bucks Rock Work Camp, which in retrospect sounds like a prison. Nevertheless, we had been good friends. Naturally, I was quite surprised to see him at a Miles Davis concert where he performed with one of his electrified ensembles. Since the venue for this concert was near a bar in Baltimore called The Club Charles-we decided to go there for a slow libation.

There are probably quite a few people who *actually* don't like going to The Club Charles. It is called the Club Charles because was and is now still located at 1724 North Charles Street. I suppose a lot of people like going there. However, I have a rather blasé attitude toward this watering hole simply because it doesn't have live music, it does not have a kitchen, and because it's too far from where I live. In these days of way too many drunk drivers, I eschew going where there's no kitchen. Nevertheless, it is indeed a very fine drinking establishment-and the jukebox has a top-notch selection of music. Along with that, the clientele is what you would call quite interesting and easy to chat with. On any given day you are bound to run into what some call "local characters" or "regular folk" and then fall into a lively discussion about any old thing under the sun. Oh, and the folks tending the bar are quite friendly and do not mind chatting a bit with you. So, all in all I would say that if I lived near enough to The Club Charles there is a fifty-fifty chance I might be somewhat of a regular there. What does that mean? Simply stated this place is hip-without being loud about it. Cool without being ostentatious about it. It is like Mike's Place in that Ferlinghetti poem. And above all The Club Charles is indeed one of the iconic bars in Baltimore. It is the only bar I have ever known with a nickname. However, you had better have earned your Boy/Girl Scout Merritt Badges in Hipness and Friendly Drinking before you even dare call it the Club Chuck. And earning these badges requires just these things.

1) Go there and be hip or be gone

2) Don't cop no 'tudes (That's attitudes for those of you who live in Cape Jurado)[33]

---

[33] This is parody of what the Late Rush Limbaugh said. He would always say :"For those of you in Rio Linda before explaining something that was patently obvious. In response to that this author found out that Cape Jurado was the birthplace of Rush Limbaugh.

3)Tip the bartender twenty-percent

4)Drink responsibly

With these covenants in mind, Lew Frisch and I entered the semi-lit venue known and loved by all who have bent an elbow there. The first thing on our minds was talking about the concert. The almost very first thing my buddy said was to bemoan the fact that Miles Davis did not introduce the songs or the musicians and at times turned his back on the audience.

These things set off alarm bells in my mind. I kept quiet while he told me; "Cannonball Adderly talked to the audience" I got sarcastic and replied "So what! Miles Davis hired Cannonball Adderley. That does not mean he has to *act* like Cannonball Adderley!" Then I went off a bit. First I said: "If Miles Davis had *not* turned his back to us neither of us would have seen that beautiful yellow sun on the back of his turquoise jacket. And besides both of them have seen Aaron Copland, Igor Stravinsky, and Leonard Bernstein conducting orchestras. Not only did they keep their backs turned towards us, but their wardrobes were your basic stuff. And like Miles Davis they did acknowledge the applause given at the end of their concerts."

Then I said:" Miles Davis was conducting his ensemble just like any serious conductor of music would do. Remember JAZZ is really African American Classical Music! So, Lew keep your pie hole open long enough to order us a drink."

It was then that I felt a hand on my back. And a Black man with a raspy voice whispered in my ear: "You tell him kid! Yeah you tell him kid.

Don't let him tell you any different" (or words to that effect) and with that, he patted my back and strolled out the door just seconds before a lovely bartender brought Lew and me our drinks, and said "Mister Davis told me to have one on him"

And so, we did. And that was just that.

End Piece Four

Jimmy Giuffrie Brings Down The House

Jimmy Giuffre Brings Down The House

Background information	
Birth name	James Peter Giuffre
Born	April 26, 1921
	Dallas, Texas, U.S.

Died	April 24, 2008 (aged 86) Pittsfield, Massachusetts, U.S.
Genres	<ul><li>Jazz</li><li>free jazz</li><li>West Coast jazz</li><li>cool jazz</li><li>folk jazz</li><li>chamber jazz</li><li>third stream</li></ul>
Occupation(s)	Musician, composer, arranger
Instrument(s)	Clarinet, tenor saxophone, baritone saxophone
Years active	The 1940s–1990s
Labels	Capitol, Atlantic, Verve, Choi

Someone, not me though could write a real book about the multi-instrumentalist/composer/arranger/ensemble unit leader Jimmy Giuffre. However, this effort at this time would take up volumes. However, in the interests of brevity, these few sentences should do the trick. The first time I had heard about Jimmy Giuffrie was when I discovered Third - Stream music. Third- Stream Music was an attempt to merge classical as in European Classical Music with Jazz. Aside from the innovators, Gunther Schuler, John Lewis, and Jimmy Giuffre none of the other members of this musical sub-group ever made much of an impression on me. And, for the life of me, I can't remember any other Third-Stream advocates.

I do however remember Jimmy Giuffrie was a friend of a teacher of mine from India named Sushil Mukherjee. This teacher of mine was a local hero in the small Lennox/Stockbridge Jazz community. So, it was not unusual to go by his house and see other musicians having dinner there or jam sessions or both. In one of these get-togethers with the students at my school (Windsor Mountain), I met Mr. Giuffrie who was asking Sushil Mukherjee if he knew any way he could use some Indian yoga method to enable him to play the clarinet from the bell up as opposed to the traditional way of playing the clarinet from the mouthpiece down.

However, to quote a lyric of a song by Jerry Ragovoy that Paul Butterfield made sort of famous:" That was a long time ago" Now let's fast forward to Baltimore somewhere in the mid-seventies. It was on one of those Sunday afternoons at three in the afternoon at the Famous Ballroom. It was in the autumn of one of those years perhaps 1975-I can't rightly remember the exact day. However, I do remember the featured artist at the Famous was the Jimmy Giuffrie Quintet.

From the minute these five men went on stage, I knew this was going to be one of those make or break it shows. This was for two reasons. The first one was aside from the contrabass performer Bob Cunningham the rest of the band was white. Not only were they white-but they were old white men. However, this did not dissuade these stalwart musicians/composers from tuning up. It also did not stop Jimmy Giuffrie from announcing the first song. As I remember he said "We'd like to start off this set with a composition by a good friend of our band the great African -American saxophonist Eddie Harris called Freedom Jazz Dance. With those words and someone shouting out something like "damn that cat knows his Jazz" The show began. This was a magical show. Each song built on the good music of the previous composition. Each solo was greeted with the enthusiastic response reserved for Jazz Royalty. When a member of the audience yelled out: "Give the drummer some" Jimmy Giuffrie called out Night in Tunisia and Bobby Rosengarten went to work on those tubs as if he was channeling Art Blakey. He played like a man possessed with the love of Jazz and this was his last day on this planet to show it. The crowd went t-totally wild. Not only that but when this white drummer said after the composition: "I need to publicly thank my personal Jazz hero Art Blakey for giving me the inspiration to be where I am today!", he got a standing O. (That's a standing ovation for all of you in Cape Jurado) With scattered shouts of "that brother knows his –stuff" The music went on. When someone else called out:" Give the bass a taste" Jimmy Giuffrie and his quintet did Body and Soul-and Bob Cunningham did a bowed bass solo that sent chills all over all of us. It started out with the piano and bass backing him up-then after he soloed a while the band came back to play the theme. However just as all of us thought the song was finished Bob

Cunningham went into a solo arco (bowed) coda that put time on hold and quieted the room down so much you could hear in the words of the great African -American poet Kenneth Carroll "hear a dollar bill fall on cotton" once again the patrons rose to their feet just clapping and cheering for this performance. This was supposed to be the final song of the final set. But the audience was having none of that. First one then more yelled out "encore-?one more song" etc. What could Jimmy Giuffrie do? Heck, even the few Black Cultural -Nationalists who had an uneasy truce with the rest of this multi-cultural crowd were slapping fives and yelling out "Play the blues we can use!" As I said earlier what could Jimmy Giuffrie do? He had the whole audience in the palm 0of his hand-and he was not about to blow it. So, with a nod from the master of ceremonies a cat named Vernon (I forgot his last name), the band went into a medium-tempo blues. First Bob Brookmeyer the valve trombonist did a sort of gutbucket solo that elicited thunderous applause. Then Russ Freedman launched into a solo with block chords that just made the piano ring out with joy-to the joy of all who were listening. Then Jimmy Giuffrie stepped up to the mic clarinet in hand and motioned for the rest of the group to lay out. Then as a respectful silence descended upon all of us Jimmy Giuffrie began his solo. At first, it was what would be called a few noodles-then a few more-. Have you ever been outside just before a big rainstorm? You know it just doesn't start raining all at once. You know there are a few raindrops that will fall on the ground them more-and more then when you think this will be a small sprinkle the clouds will tell you this is cloudburst time. And so it was that night. First came the clarinet noodlings. Then Bob Cunningham began to do a sort of hesitant walking bass back up, that gradually picked up steam until Bobby Rosengarten started in on what was a sure-enough funky back beat accompaniment that gave the pianist Russ Freedman permission to play some strong block chord accompaniments. What could Jimmy Giuffrie do? He did what any good Jazz soloist would do! He turned on the heat and went to cooking. And cook he did. With each and every chorus he cooked and cooked and cooked. Then something truly magical happened. It started off in the corner of the room where the dashiki-clad African -American cultural nationalists would sit. To this day I do not know who it was. Perhaps it was the fellow named Yusef Bey or his mentor Ronald Hicks-El. I can't remember. However, these cats started clapping in rhythm in rhythm to the music in the traditional sign that means "don't stop now-bro". Then one by one the rest of us began clapping. And clap we did as if we were one big percussion section clapping on the traditional one and three beats of the song. After a bit I saw one fine matronly looking elderly African -American Queen dressed to "The Tens" (One step above "Dressed to the "nines") Get up in her fox fur coat and start to shimmy like he sister Kate with her elegantly dressed patron dressed in the finest pin-striped three-piece suit replete with white spats. Then a couple of white Maryland Institute College of Art students who looked like they could have been at a Grateful Dead show started strutting their stuff in the best jitterbug style. And that was all it took. Soon everyone who had legs and a place to dance were doing just that. Some were dancing the jitterbug-others were doing that kind of embrace and release dance ballroom dancers do, others were doing a kind of back-and-forth shuffle, while still others were just standing in place - their hands in the air doing that hallelujah praise Jesus kind of sway that ladies in the Black Church do in what James Baldwin called: The Amen Corner". Even the hippies got into the act doing what I call the hair-waving-Woodstock dance. Even I joined in after a young woman I just did not know took me by the handout onto a crowded dance floor. And above all this twirling and swirling Jimmy Giuffrie was blowing in the words of Chuck Berry "like a hurricane" with Bobby Brookmeyer riffing in the back as if he was a full-blown horn section.

There was so much positive energy in the room that if it were electricity it could provide enough natural energy to wean the world off fossil fuels for decades and have Arabian oil sheiks standing outside the United Nations like scalpers at a concert trying to ticket and getting not one taker to buy their oil. Lord knows how long the legs kept shaking. However, shake they did. Then as much as everyone would have loved to strut their stuff even after the cows came home-Jimmy Giuffrie brought the song to a nice close that left all of us looking for the remainders of the rug we had cut to shreds. After getting a five-minute standing On the five men did a hand-holding bow (or two) and strutted off the stage like Super Bowl champs. Quite soon thereafter Vernon said it was time to go. And leave we did with each of us feeling sanctified or groovy or just plain hog-happy down the big wide stairs of the Famous with enough memories to last at least on life plus one resurrection onto another Balmy Baltimore autumnal evening ready as we would ever be to go, home cop, some Z's and get ready for our day jobs or whatever we had to do in the upcoming week.

End Piece Four

APPENDIX

Four Poems on Space

Listening to Sun Ra At The Famous Ball Room

"What is that sound?

Sounds like thunder" Laurie Anderson

Yes, the sound sounds like thunder

Sounds like a space age drum and bugle corp.

Sounds like heavenly horns

Sounds like Sun Ra

Sounds like Sun Ra and his solar ARCHESTRA

Can you hear the space porter calling out?

"Rocket number nine

Rocket number nine

All aboard"

When listening to Sun Ra

We travel the space ways

We never leave our chairs

But we are traveling the space ways

Yes, it's true

Listening to Sun Ra

The saying is really true.

SPACE IS THE PLACE

Sun Ra

Sun Ra, c. 1973

CHAPTER SIXTEEN

End Piece Five

From Bits And Pieces

By this Author

I Remember the Famous Ballroom

W. N. E. W. had the make-believe ballroom

But

B'more had

THE FAMOUS BALLROOM

And that was the REAL DEAL

And

When after some of us had finished being saved at church

And

Others of us had just finished lunch

All of us went to

The FAMOUS BALLROOM to get sanctified in the sound of surprise

Or jazz for all you L 7s

Sunday afternoons we strode up those 39 steps

(or more?)

Dressed in our Sunday best

Or our thrift store best

Or something in between

We brought our best attitudes/vibes or whatever and were prepared to deal with amazement

With a capital A

This was the place where jazz lovers of every size shape race and age mixed and mingled

We called this place The FAMOUS

(Why use too many words)

To us it was the FAMOUS

(And if you had to ask-you'd never know)

This was a place that if you dug the music

You knew you belonged

(You did not have to ask)

It was strangers first then friends second.

Here under the stars painted on the celling and by the Wall of Fame

We watched

Coltrane beating his chest because he had

"Run out of saxophone"

After playing the bag pipes

Jimmy Giuffrie playing the blues and getting the whole place a-rockin'

Joe Chambers play the musical saw

Sun Ra tell us SPACE WAS THE PLACE

Archie Shepp play Along Came Betty

And Arthur and Red Prysock play pretty for the ladies

And Sarah Vaughn and a host of other divas sing sexy for the men folks

We sat in folding chairs

Or in round tables

Talking jazz

And eating some of the finest soul food under God's Blue Sky that was guaranteed to put hair on the chests of the men and take hair off the legs of women

Guaranteed to make you live forever or you got your money back.

Clark Terry mumbled

Or

Cleanhead Vinton sang

"I want a little girl"

And someone yelled

"You don't need a little girl pops-you need a nurse"

This was Sunday at the Famous

And it was taken in good stride

No one was offended by the shouts of

"Give the drummer some"

"Give the bass a tase'"

This was not some Sophisticated High Brow affair

The stars and the listeners chit chatted gave autographs on the newly purchased records

Over ribs or chicken or the hooch b that was in b. y. o. b

We talked jazz

We talked jazz

WE TALKED JAZZ

We knew who Elvin was and who Max was and others

We argued the pros and cons of the new electric Miles Davis Band

Then we were quiet as church mice

Chic Corea or Red Garland or Jessica Williams made the piano come alive

Gracham Moncour the 3rd made that trombone moan

And Sonny Rollins took us to Saint Thomas

AND MEMORIES WERE MADE

The Big Book About Sounds

And as the sun went down

And a blue moon came out to play

We all went home

Happy as hogs

Pleased as peacocks

And ready to face blue Monday with the music still in our heads and
yes

Smiles still on our faces

(A Colombo Coda

By the way just one or two more things

Where did they get those cardboard serving bowls they put ice or
chips in

And

Do they still make Suburban Club Soda?)

CHAPTER SEVENTEEN

MILES DAVIS FAMOUS Ballroom Baltimore

MILES DAVIS FAMOUS Ballroom Baltimore Cardstock Concert Poster
12x18 £8.59 - Picklocks UK

picclick.co.uk

Merchandise - baltimorejazz.com

End Piece Six

From Shipyard Days And Nights

By This Author

Baltimore Has Its Share of Characters And Heroes

Some Brief Sketches

The casual observer might think that other than John Watters the city of Baltimore has no interesting characters. That my friend is far from the truth. The problem is that no one knows about these folks. That is why I am going to tell you about a few of the more colorful individuals that I have been pleased to have known

1)
tENTATIVELY a cONVIENIENCE
AKA "TENT"

You want to know this sound thinker, raconteur, and all- around good guy's real name? Look it up. Why should I spill the beans

This fellow personifies performance art to the utmost. His whole being is art. From the three-dimensional tattoo on the top of his brain, to the soles of his feet under a pair of pants made entirely out of zippers this man is the very living embodiment of the human spirit unchained.

To do true justice to this person would take volumes of books. If you Google his name you will find out all you want to know about him. However, I do know about his various events like his events in the tunnels of Baltimore or his film Piss on Bob's Head. I have heard a rumor that Tent somehow snuck into Buckingham Palace and made off with a turd belonging to Queen Elizabeth -but I would have to say that under the most lazy cross examining in court my case would be flimsy at best.

With this in mind, I do know that whatever Tent has and will do, it will have the stamp of total originality about it. Whether it is his proposal for

New York and Baltimore to switch names in order to make Baltimore Artists better known or the fact that he was once arrested and charged with violating a law that was not on the books, nothing or no one can hold a candle to Tent and the successful antics he so skillfully pulled off.

Neil Feather

Like the old Yankee tinkerer Neil Feather tinkers and creates his own music on his own musical instruments. This composer/sculpture maker does his magic in the style of Harry Parch or Earl Brown or Moondog, or the great master John Cage, Neil Feather tinkers and fiddles and composes until the results are fascinating. It's composers like him that make me wish I had more talent in making music and making musical things

Albert Dailey

Sadly, enough I only heard this Jazz pianist/composer perform once at the Famous Ballroom. A portion of this stellar performance was recorded on the Milestone Label it's called Home. I am not the only one who had the pleasure of hearing Albert Dailey. A former ensemble leader of his Gary Bartz told me that even though he had the good fortune and pleasure of performing and recording with some of the stellar members of the Jazz community such as McCoy Tyner and Keith Jarrett he felt that the times he spent with Albert Daily were the times he treasured the most. With those kind of props who could argue with him.

Gary Bartz

Let me put it to you "country simple" as William S. Burroughs would say. Gary Bartz sets the standard for the modern woodwind Jazz composer/musician. When listening to him I hear a sound that is like a combination of Sonny Rollins, Louis Jordan and uncapurability of pure genius. I have heard him take what would be a dribble of unconnected notes and make a gorgeous composition out of these seemingly unconnected notes. His recorded versions of the Smoky Robinson composition and My Funny Valentine still rank as favorite covers of these standards. I really love the song I've Known Rivers that he dedicated to Langston Hughes. Oh, and yes I do think fondly and thank Miles Davis for recording and performing with this charming musical charm from Charm City

As you might have noticed I have signed my name Alan Herbert Rowan Baptiste Barysh. My name after I had it changed was Alan Herbert Barysh. It would have stayed Alan Herbert Barysh forever. However, two things happened in my life that caused me to add the extra middle names.

The first was the death of Rowan Rauche the daughter of Heather Rauche. Let me go into more detail. Heather Rauche and I are Facebook friends. I don't know much about her. I do know that she was "with child" when we became cyberspace friends. I also knew that she was peacock proud to be pregnant. As a matter of fact, I would say she was delirious with her pregnancy. She was delirious with the joy of having a new baby. From what I saw in her Facebook posts, she was truly celebrating her pregnancy.

As others did, I followed her posts on Facebook. Then I learned the truth. Or rather the sad truth. It was just two hours after Heather Rauche gave birth that her baby died. When I heard the news I felt like someone had punched me in the gut. I thought how hard it must have been to lose a child that early in that child's life. I knew I had to do something about it. The first thing I did was to send her daily posts of encouraging messages. I vowed to keep sending these posts until asked to stop. These posts were to counter the bogus words of "concern" like "She's better off now" and "Well at least she won't have to suffer now" ad nauseam. It's good that these faux counselors were not near me. These would have been replies. "How on earth do you know this child is in a better place? Did you visit her? Did she call you?" Or yeah right that's some kind of consolation. Then there was the callous remark "This too shall pass. You will get over it" To these bogus remarks of concern these are two of my better sarcastic remarks. Who are you? Are you the shift supervisor for Mourners Incorporated? What are you saying? Are you telling me that there's only an allotted amount of time for mourning? Then there's the "Oh well---that's life" response. To that, I say that's because you are letting life run you. No, we shouldn't let life run us. We should run life. Right now, we don't have the medical resources or skills to make life run for us. That doesn't mean that we can't work to change things. That means that each and every person must work to create a world where no child dies a child and no one dies needlessly. In that spirit, I added Rowan to my name so that wherever I go I will keep her legacy alive.

I added Baptiste to my name in honor of a brother of a caregiver here at Beechwood Assisted Living. Once again something gut-punched me. I could not fathom losing a sibling. This death was doubly devastating. The tragedy of having this happen to a woman who devotes her whole working life to servicing the people who live here brought out the best in me. So, asked her if I could incorporate the name of her brother in my name and keep her brother's name as his legacy wherever I went and work for the day when sisters and brothers don't have to bury their kin before they die or go on living without knowing that there's someone in their corner who can lift some of the burden of grief from their shoulders.

Now for the lighter news. For a while now I have noticed that the placing of initials after the name of someone denotes an appreciation of the things they have accomplished in their life. You know like PhD or MD etc. So, I decided to throw some initials after my name. I chose M E O B for Most Extraordinary Old Buzzard/ And now even Paul Harvey knows the rest of the story.

Thanks for dropping by

May I shown to the door?

Portrait of the author with Jeff Patterson the first marine to refuse to fight in the first Persian Gulf War/Invasion

Portrait of the author in almost -living color

Portrait of the author in living black and white

No One Can Be You But You!

No one can tell the story of your life
In the first person
Better than you!
No one can sing the song you sing
The dance you dance
The self-portrait you create
The kiss you kiss
Or
The gifts you give from your heart
Others may try
Others will fail
That's *their* problem
Others may tell better stories
Others may sing better songs
Others may dance better than you
Others may make better self-portraits than you
Others may kiss others better than you
Other hearts may give better gifts than your heart can purchase
That's okay
Go ahead
Be you
Be unique
Be so priceless and wonderous that even Sotheby's
can't put a price tag on it
Think about this
You are the only one

Who can make your best foot be
That best foot forward
That good first impression
That last pleasant memory
That lasting impression/memory
That you have chiseled in the stone of time
Ponder upon this
If you know you have tried to share the best but you think your best
Just
Won't
Cut
It
Take a moment to listen to
Your New Jersey Poetic Muse
When the muse
Says: "Don't drive yourself nuts!
Fa-get about it
Ya keep worryin' 'bout it
Ya gonna drive your self
Straight into da nut-house
Like I said
You keep worrying about
Ya gonna drive yourself nuts!
So fa-get about it"
And when you are done pondering
Keep this in mind
Snowflakes don't have twin siblings!

About the Author

Alan Barysh is a writer, poet, performance poet, and musician. He is a graduate of Windsor Mountain School, and The Broadcasting Institute of Maryland Between. 1966 and in1989 he performed and or conducted for Albert Ayler and John Cage. In 1998 he was Poet In Residence at The Maryland Institute College of Art. In 1987, he was a featured reader at Art Scape. In 2007 he was a featured reader at the Maryland Book Festival

Two collections of short stories Mike And Maryanne Meet The Angel Of Death, and the sequel Upon Awakening Father Brown Finds A Solution, were published by ApozathyPress His own self-published books are: Bugged, Slugged, Mugged, Art Between Deliveries, The Wit And Wisdom Of Donald Trump, 5-7-6-365, 5-7-5=365, Poems For The Universe/Space Haiku, and John Cage On The Download, He has also appeared in Octopus Dreams an anthology edited by Julie Fisher, and Blu Magazine of The Breuderhoff Religious Community.

His self-produced compact discs are Resist To Exist, Alan Barysh With The Buzzard Luck Ensemble, and Art Between Deliveries. He is featured on two compact disks of poetry by Blair Ewing. They are Word Up Baltimore and The Road Less Traveled. He has written The Adventures of Huckleberry Finn without racist words and faux radio advertisements as a radio play. He is currently writing new versions of the Nancy Drew mystery series. The Nancy Drew in this reincarnation . smokes weed, drinks margaritas, cusses like a sailor, has a live-in boyfriend and was a former member of the revolutionary group Students For A Democratic Society,

For more information and or interviews you may write

Alan Barysh
101 North Beechwood Avenue
Catonsville Maryland 21228
Phone 443-239-5325
e-mail magoo1917 earthlink.net